Kairos Care

Aaron Perry

KAIROS CARE

A Process for Pastoral
Counseling in the Office and
in Everyday Encounters

Nashville

KAIROS CARE:
A PROCESS FOR PASTORAL COUNSELING IN THE OFFICE
AND IN EVERYDAY ENCOUNTERS

Copyright © 2021 by Abingdon Press

All rights reserved.
No part of this work may be reproduced or transmitted in any form or by any means, electronic or mechanical, including photocopying and recording, or by any information storage or retrieval system, except as may be expressly permitted by the 1976 Copyright Act or in writing from the publisher. Requests for permission should be addressed to Permissions, Abingdon Press, 2222 Rosa L. Parks Boulevard, Nashville, TN 37228-1306, or permissions@abingdonpress.com.

Library of Congress Control Number: 2021935507
ISBN: 978-1-5018-9911-9

Scripture quotations unless noted otherwise are from the Common English Bible. Copyright © 2011 by the Common English Bible. All rights reserved. Used by permission. www.CommonEnglishBible.com.

Scripture quotations marked (NIV) are taken from the Holy Bible, New International Version®, NIV®. Copyright © 1973, 1978, 1984, 2011 by Biblica, Inc.™ Used by permission of Zondervan. All rights reserved worldwide. www.zondervan.com The "NIV" and "New International Version" are trademarks registered in the United States Patent and Trademark Office by Biblica, Inc.™

21 22 23 24 25 26 27 28 29 30—10 9 8 7 6 5 4 3 2 1
MANUFACTURED IN THE UNITED STATES OF AMERICA

Contents

vii	Introduction
1	Chapter 1: The Model
25	Chapter 2: Look and Listen
43	Chapter 3: Clarify
57	Chapter 4: Conference
77	Chapter 5: Statement of Change
87	Chapter 6: Plan
105	Chapter 7: Action and Accountability
123	Chapter 8: Follow Up
137	Notes

Introduction

Coffee, Counsel, Incarnation

"Starbucks?"[1] The text message came in the early evening from a friend inviting me out for some unnecessary caffeine. Perhaps my children were asleep—likely they weren't—but my wife still encouraged me to skip out to share a warm drink with my friend. We chatted briefly, light conversation matching the aroma of light roast. Then his hands doubled around his coffee and his shoulders leaned in. They didn't slump with discouragement; they were stressed with determination. Something was on his mind and his mission was to remove it.

"Should I start my own business?"

It's an exciting, multi-layered question, but from this friend at this time, there was less excitement and more layers. He was a carpenter working for a family member in the same field: a family member he loved and respected. An entrepreneurial step would be a family issue, but of what kind? A new business could be seen as a kind of *pregnancy* with shared excitement all the way around; it could be seen as a teenager *leaving home for college*, spreading his wings and validating the tutelage of his elders, even if there was a measure of sentimentality; it could be seen as a *divorce*, a rupture that sent out relational ripples.

As I leaned back in my chair to begin framing some questions to reveal any potential wider context, I realized: "He's asking me because I'm his pastor." This was a pastoral counseling session, sprung upon me right in the middle of a Starbucks. Privacy was ignored and interruptions were likely—but pastoral counseling it was. I wasn't frustrated or annoyed or anything of the sort. This is what pastors do. Yes, we were friends, but in this moment, I was his pastor.

Pastors Counsel in the Every Day

I'm a pastor and still think of myself as a pastor after becoming a professor. I've listened through thousands of hours of counseling as a pastor, many engagements like what would emerge over the next two hours in the coffee shop. I'm neither a licensed pastoral counselor nor a professional counselor. Pastoral counseling still leaves me with some uneasiness and a bit of trepidation. I think of myself as a pastor; I don't think of myself as a counselor. My counseling training in seminary happened through a variety of lectures and readings, but since I was studying theology specifically, counseling curriculum wasn't required. Further back, my pastoral ministries undergraduate degree provided helpful, basic, and (in some ways) sufficient pastoral counseling training, but once in pastoral ministry what was helpful, basic, and sufficient quickly needed to be harnessed, boosted, and supplemented. Suddenly what I knew wasn't enough, and what I knew needed to be owned and applied in the moment. Being seated across the table from someone in a family affair—whether starting a new business or recovering from marital infidelity—forced me to deploy skills quickly and, only by God's grace, effectively. But even while I thought of myself as a pastor and not as a counselor, those Starbucks moments were times of pastoral responsibility. The pastor was called upon, and God deploys the pastor for those times.

The pastoral calling demands nothing less than our best in these "sprung-upon" moments, whether they happen in a coffee shop, grocery stores, offices, car rides, or homes. These moments come. And they are not to be scorned. They are *incarnational* moments. Incarnational theology is not simply about God taking on flesh but God taking on the everydayness of life. God, in Christ, lived in the *rhythms* of bodily life. Pastors are not simply bodies in offices but persons in the rhythm of life with God's people, offering counsel in the ordinariness of life. Incarnational ministry happens wherever pastors are found alongside their parishioners.

Pastoral counseling is often incarnational ministry in impromptu conversation. Sometimes it happens through a set of structured meetings. Either way, these vital conversations must be handled responsibly to model incarnation appropriately. If pastoral counsel doesn't take place in these moments, it might not happen at all. The void will be filled—perhaps well and perhaps poorly. Social media, fools, and the soul's enemy are all eager and waiting to help form the souls of your people. Access to Christian counseling may or may not be accessible, but it's not likely to get *more accessible* and so you will be even more necessary. Pastor, you're on call.

Now, let's quickly assuage a potential concern: When we talk about impromptu conversations or coffee shop moments, we are *not* talking about dropping professional boundaries. A pastor is never to be what Stanley Hauerwas calls a "quivering mass of availability."[2] We are *not* talking about going into full-on crisis counseling for every faux-crisis. We are *not* talking about jumping to attention, canceling vacation, and running out on family dinner every time the phone rings, buzzes, pops, squeals, or whatever other indicating alert it produces.

Let's draw some wisdom from John Wesley. In his sermon "The Good Steward," Wesley says we should use our financial resources in the following way: first, care for you and your family; second, give it to God by caring for others.[3] While Wesley is speaking of financial resources and other tangible goods, we might also consider emotional resources. You are not always at your best for your church. Neither can you *only* be at your best for your family and closest friends. However, if your family and closest friends are not consistently getting quality attention and care, then something is out of order.

What we *are* talking about is being in the rhythm of life with your people—including family and others in your spiritual care; moments when you know God is stirring, God's Spirit is active, and that God has placed a pastor on the scene with one of God's people—whether it is a structured appointment or an impromptu java. These are moments of pastoral counseling that must be handled with depth and skill—even if you think of yourself as a pastor and not as a counselor.

Every Pastor Is a Counselor

Sitting in Starbucks with my friend as his pastor helped to clarify my understanding of pastoral counseling. I saw myself offering pastoral counsel in the same way that a relatively well-educated (in theology, Bible, and humanities) friend offers spiritually sensitive, loyal, and interested wisdom. If a problem needs more support than what this relatively well-educated friend can provide, then the pastor should consider referring the parishioner. (We will address referral more in depth next chapter.) I also started thinking of pastoral counseling as making and deepening friendships. While I'm not best friends with all my friends, I have found relational stability with a variety of depths across many friends. These two frames—pastoral counseling as an interested friend and as a friend-making practice—helped me to broaden and refine my pastoral counseling.

Re-framing pastoral counseling is one of the joys of teaching active pastors. I have found that pastoral counseling can be daunting to some—they fear they could never do it well! And I have found that pastoral counseling can be scorned by others—they aren't called to do *that* work. Pastoral counseling is seen either as too difficult, requiring specialized training, advanced degrees, and hours of clinical observation, or as too soft, too disconnected from the apostolic ministry of pastors who must be meeting with strong leaders and lost souls to drive the vision of the church and grow its influence every waking moment of the workday.

Earning the Privilege of Counseling

Some people aren't discerning in their friendships. It's why we should teach this proverb: "befriend fools and get in trouble" (Prov 13:20 CEB). To those tempted to take the counsel of the fool, the pastor needs to present a

Introduction

ready alternative. They need to present as one who is wise. The pastor needs to be seen as trustworthy before they will be trusted—especially by many people who want to impress their pastor or protect their reputation with a friend. In other words, pastor, you earn the privilege of providing counsel. In a day gone by, people may have given the office of the pastor a measure of automatic respect. And to be sure, some people still do. But others will need to see evidence that you can help them.

And this takes intentionality. During my college days, I was doing an impersonation for a group of friends. As a political cartoon will emphasize unique features of the politician it is depicting, I was keying in on signature elements of the voice I was impersonating. I was trying for some laughs without considering the consequences. It was a defining moment for me. One of my mentors, a dean at the school, gently took me aside and said, "Aaron, you will never know who *won't* come and entrust themselves to you because of the way you just spoke." The opportunity to make an impression often presents itself in secret. We don't always know when we are pressing our own image into the mind of another—someone who is watching, testing, considering entrusting their own self to you.

Now, there's a balance to be maintained here. Think of the gymnast who has strength to hold herself in balance between two suspended rings or on a narrow beam of wood. She needs tremendous power to hold herself in balance because there are forces pulling in other directions. The balance to be maintained when forming your image in the mind of another is between apathy and scrutiny. On the one hand, there are people who care little what others think of them and do not moderate their behavior at all. They might respond to the dean who warned me by saying, "Who cares what they think? I am who I am. If they want to talk to me, they should know who I am." On the other hand, there are people who care too much what others think of them and experience a kind of paralysis. They might not risk so much as a friendly knock-knock joke for fear of whom it might offend.

The balance between these two extremes takes strength. I suggest growing in five factors to build your strength to maintain this balance when earning the privilege of the counselor and trusted friend:

1. **Passion:** If you're not a sports person, you likely don't understand the passion a fan has for a football or baseball or hockey team. If you're not a music lover, you likely don't understand the passion a musician has for high-quality sound equipment. Passion is enthusiasm. People need to know that you can appreciate their passion for a subject or issue before they can trust you. The word *passion* still includes suffering among its definitions, and so it is important to keep suffering in mind. While sports and even music might be fairly benign examples, our people are wrestling with issues that are very important—ones that have been filled with suffering. They need to know that the pastor takes things seriously, that the pastor can be passionate about a subject, even recognizing that it has been a context involving suffering. Pastors earn the counseling opportunity by showing passion.

2. **Empathy:** But passion can't be the only factor. Too many Facebook fights emerge around important topics because people only bring *one* factor: passion. Pastors must show empathy in addition to passion. Some people will only trust the pastor if they are confident the pastor has worked to understand a subject from a variety of angles. Critical thinking skills are not the same as neutrality; in many situations a pastor should *not* be neutral. But the wise pastor seeks to know the experience and rationale of a variety of people on important subjects. Pastors earn the counseling opportunity by showing empathy.

3. **Gentleness:** Early in my ministry, I preached a sermon that I can't remember. I doubt anyone remembers it. What I can remember, however, was the response of a parishioner when he came to see me the next day. He wanted a fight. *And I gave him one.* People will triangulate fighters—they will try to get them on their side against someone else—but they don't often seek them out for counsel. I failed my parishioner the day I mirrored his fighting spirit. Pastors earn the counseling opportunity by showing gentleness.

4. **Humility:** Sometimes people will say, "I'm just the same as everybody else." I hope that's not the case. Especially for a person who believes in sanctification. The person God has justified and is sanctifying is *not* the same as everybody else. If pastors are the very same as everyone else, then they likely have nothing of value to offer. Humility is recognizing that the deep challenges that all our people face—illness, divorce, shame, addiction, greed, and so on—are challenges to which we are susceptible, as well. The pastor's life is redeemed and is being sanctified, but it is not bulletproof and infallible. Pastors earn the counseling opportunity by showing humility.

5. **Intelligence:** The pastor must be a person whom others are confident is well-researched, reflective, and resourceful on important subjects. It is not enough to have an opinion. This doesn't mean you don't have an angle, but there's a difference between a person who has an opinion and a person who has an informed point of view. Pastors earn the counseling opportunity by showing they are intelligent and informed.

Appreciating the Counseling Opportunity

In the era of streaming television and movies, it's common for many viewers to watch a full season in two to three weeks or even less time. As a result, viewers cover lots of the program's plot relatively quickly. One of the benefits of this immersion is that the story can be followed really closely. Characters aren't forgotten and themes aren't lost. At the same time, there might be an unexpected redundancy. Sometimes around the middle of season three or four, we realize, "They have been showing the same episode over and over again." The plot doesn't move. It just circles back. The characters end up in the same trials and love triangles. Whereas viewers used to be wide awake and on the edge of their seats, they're now sleeping with eyes open, shoulders slouched. The show might even have become background noise to something more engaging.

The same thing can happen with our everyday lives. It's the same characters and the same plot. But here's the difference: If you're in leadership, especially pastoral leadership, then there's enough tension and drama to keep you engaged, but you can forget the multiple story lines happening around you. We miss that the same episode is happening over and over again. We become caught up in a story that isn't advancing.

It's no secret that as people rise through an organization, they lose connection with those without the same power and privilege. "Leadership is often accompanied by privileges and choices that enable the leaders to escape the challenges and struggles of ordinary folks."[4] When these two phenomena come together—becoming blind to our context and limited in our interactions—then we have double blindness. We are blind to our own context and unaware that there is a wider context around us. What this looks like with pastors is a disconnect from the everyday life of many persons whose soul is in their care.[5] When pastors are not experiencing and hearing the stories of death, illness, trauma, birth, marriage, divorce, aging, getting fired or laid off, moving out, and moving on, they are missing the depth of incarnation in the everyday of life.

When parishioners speak to the pastor about these issues, it is not only the parishioner who is helped. The pastor is kept grounded in the life of the church. The pastor is given a chance to practice and hone essential skills such as listening, asking open-ended questions, crafting and revising plans, empathizing, and displaying an authentic persona. These skills never go out of style and are not limited to just a few church contexts.

Seizing the Moment

But these everyday conversations, whether in the office or the coffee shop, do not always feel so meaningful. Two interventions can overcome the drift and disinterest that blocks pastoral care. First, a well-formed theological imagination helps us to see God at work when the pastor does this work.

Introduction

Second, a natural counseling structure can help the pastor to navigate what can often be intimidating and unclear. A pastoral theology guides the pastor when they are unsure that any good is happening, and a structure helps some good to be done.

The joy of making friends, the humility of seeing my limits as a pastoral counselor, and the desire to be an effective guide in the moment helped me develop a model of pastoral counseling that is portable and applicable across multiple contexts. It can be used to establish a series of time-limited pastoral counseling sessions, and it can be used to navigate a single conversation that erupts in the moment. It easily adopts key insights from psychology, reminds us of basic pastoral counsel and care practices, and it prompts helpful assessment and position markers along the way. I hope that the distracted see the necessity and the skeptics see the possibility of faithful pastoral counsel in the everyday.

I am not a professional pastoral psychologist. While this may trigger some caution among specialists, it also offers hope to front-line pastors. I'm offering a model that is easily understood and applied—especially by those who see themselves as pastors but not as pastoral counselors. At the same time, I don't want to suggest it is without professional support or experiential testing. It emerged from my academic training in pastoral ministry, theology, and leadership. It was tested in the pastorate. If you are a pastor who doesn't consider yourself a pastoral counselor, this book is for you.

Chapter 1

The Model

Good ideas spread and good ideas last. I think this chapter has a good idea. I can say that, humbly, because its main idea is not mine. It was shared with me in a brainstorm session for a different project. It wasn't unique to the person who shared it, either. I soon found variations of it all over the web. It's been around a while. I have used it to develop a model for pastoral counsel and pastoral conversation in the everyday context of pastoral ministry, described in the introduction.

Here's what makes it shareable and durable. First, the model is easily mastered. You can access it from working memory in the "Starbucks" moment.

Second, the model acts like a storage closet. A friend of mine is colorblind. When his wife is away, she doesn't need to set out prearranged outfits because his closet is already organized according to types, colors, and patterns. When something is purchased, it's easy (for her) to see where it goes. When she's not there, my friend can pick out a great outfit easily. It's also easy to tell where the modest wardrobe might be in need. Just as a closet stores suits, shirts, and shorts, the counseling model stores a variety of theological content, leadership skills, and biblical stories. When you come across something meaningful in your ongoing education, reflection, and devotion, it's easy to see where you might store this new resource. After using it for some time, you will also see what resources you might want to add to your counseling closet.

Chapter 1

Third, the model is easily tweaked to fit the pastor's own context and purposes. Let's flesh this out with an example. I use a specific homiletical form for most of my sermons. I became more familiar with the form by drawing the diagram out and keeping the visual in front of me in my office. I would write little insights on the diagram and then try the modifications out in new sermons. Eventually, I had my own homiletical model developed from the original. Try doing the same with this model. I suggest copying the model onto a sheet of (digital) paper that you tuck inside the back of this book, tack up on a board in your office, or store on your phone. As you try the model out, add insights and reflections to make your own version. As you find yourself practicing it your own way, redraw the model to be even more personally relevant.

Learning to Tell Timing

Let's dive into the model by reflecting on two kinds of time. First, there is chronological time. This is time that keeps on ticking; it can't be stopped. Seconds turn into minutes, minutes turn into hours, hours into days, and so on. Second, there are *moments in time*, moments that stay close to our memories, imaginations, and senses; times about which we say, "It feels like it was yesterday!" These are indelible moments pressed into the memory and recalled instantly, even long past. While time keeps on ticking, some moments in time are charged with *significance and opportunity*. This is *kairos* time.

So let's start drawing a diagram. (You can find much of this diagram online. I am drawing a modified form.)

Chronological Time and the Kairos Moment

The Model

A kairos moment is placed on the chronological time line. Kairos moments can be instants or seasons of life. Without kairos moments, time keeps marching on without meaningful change. *And without due attention, work, and support at the kairos moment, life will keep on marching, as well.* That is, when a kairos moment (or season) is ignored or insufficiently attended to, life does not change. Think of the resolve that is strong on January 2 but not so much on January 22. There was a moment in time for a fresh start, but nothing happened.

Sensing a kairos moment takes discernment. It's not easy to tell if a parishioner is in such a charged moment. One of the best ways to strengthen discernment is to build margin into your schedule. Plan for interruptible time and let God fill it. This is different from planning and guarding downtime—like days off and Sabbaths. This is planned, unguarded, interruptible time; time intentionally left unfilled specifically for God to fill (or not) with divine interruptions. Building interruptible time into your schedule is the faithful flipside of believing that God is always at work in the lives of your people. If God is always at work and brings about these moments in time, God can also coordinate spiritual conversations with interruptible time.

But while planning for margin may have such coordinated coincidences, margin isn't simply about carving a consistent block or two of time every week. Margin is about *pace* throughout chronological time. Clarity and hurry are enemies; confusion and hurry are friends. Just as timing can't be hurried, the hurried often miss timing. Timing is in God's hands. We can be tempted to manufacture time and to overmanage time—to make more time for ourselves and to make more of our time. It can even be tempting to think of scheduling margin in this same spirit, but margin within chronological time is not about controlling time. It is about realizing that just as tim*ing* can't be controlled, neither can chronological *time* be controlled. We can act properly within it and be properly postured toward it. And the proper posture is humility and gratitude—humility because we aren't in control of time and gratitude because time is a gift.

The author of Ecclesiastes, the Teacher, helps us to be humble toward time. The Teacher describes everything as vapor or breath (1:2, sometimes translated "meaningless" or "pointless"). In other words, it can't be controlled.[1]

Chapter 1

Seasons for different actions come and these same seasons go (3:1-8), from the start to the end of a life. Time keeps moving, all the while giving us appropriate opportunities under the care and provision of God. When one is properly oriented to receive time, one takes delight in one's work and one's reward is what the labor produces (2:10). God has given time and provided for the worker through the labor.[2] In other words, we are humble toward time and this is what makes us able to delight in what God allows us to produce!

The longer we act as though we are in control of time, the longer we risk being crushed by the weight of this idolatry. God was instilling this principle way back in the Exodus. Just as stored manna spoiled in the jar (Exod 16:20), controlled time will ultimately be lost. The connection among time and food and seasons is clear in the parable of the foolish landowner (Luke 12:13-21). Out of the crowd, one brother calls to Jesus, complaining that his brother isn't sharing the inheritance. It's possible that the voice belongs to an older brother who has lost the inheritance by deserting his responsibility and now wants back in. It's also possible that the voice belongs to a younger brother whose older brother is not caring for his family out of the inheritance given to him. The offending brother may or may not be present in the crowd. Who knows? The context is mysterious, and Jesus is put in an impossible spot.[3] In response, Jesus avoids the arbitrator's role and instead tells the story of a foolish landowner who died the very night he had devised to store up his season's bumper crop in bigger barns. In a subsistence economy, people harvest enough for their families. The fact that this man has extra means that he has extra to provide for those who have not had a similar kind of year—or who may not have had enough for many years in a row. But the landowner does not just have extra, he has extra on top of extra! He doesn't just need barns; he needs *bigger* barns! In other words, he has enough to care for his own, set some aside, *and still has some left over!* But he has the wrong attitude about the land and toward time. He doesn't accept the fruit of the ground as a gift made possible in proper seasons. By trying to control the crop's surplus, he is trying to control the future. Contrary to the wisdom of Ecclesiastes to enjoy the fruit of work in the moment (Eccl 2:24; 3:22), the landowner is trying to control the crop and the future. As a result, he is not generous. But as a sign that he doesn't control the crops or the future, his life is lost that very night.

The Model

Rather than gratitude and generosity, there is greed and grasping. Jesus says that this is how one is when not generous toward God. It's not that God needs the food. God's initial generosity is to be reciprocated—paid forward. That's how we are formed to see the initial gift as a gift. Whichever brother is present and however the inheritance has been hoarded, humility and generosity are connected and a wise posture to adopt.

Planning interruptible times—time that can simply be used as a gift without concern—is a way to recognize that time is a gift. Such planning helps us to realize that we don't control time. We *accept* it as a gift and we *treat* it as a gift given to others, as well. This attitude positions pastors appropriately because now the fruit of pastoral labor and the proper season for caring for another can coalesce. If the timing is right, then pastors pay attention, work diligently, and give generously, just as planting and harvesting done at the appropriate times so often yields crops. If the timing is wrong, then pastors are not accountable—and can let themselves off the hook. God makes the plant grow. Proper pace keeps us from rushing about, skirting into appointments just on time, squeezing every bit of potential out of every possible moment, and it prepares us to be ready to sense and to help others sense when God is giving a *kairos* moment, a hinge in chronological time to change life's direction.

I definitely didn't have this time-posture mastered when I was caring for a congregation as a full-time pastor. I'm innately wired to grab my day with two hands and wrestle it to the ground, content only if I've gotten more done in the day than is reasonable. If I'm not going to bed wrung out, then I have left some bit of unused energy and attention in the day. This can lead to a wrong perspective on the use of time.

When I was pastoring, I could often be found rushing through the office hallways, hustling to my car to bust into a pastoral appointment just on time. No margin for red lights or rambling parishioners. On one occasion I was snagged before I reached the exit door and open air of the parking lot. A parishioner was asking for my attention. It was either listen or be late, and I couldn't be late. I remember the crestfallen demeanor of the person who just wanted to be heard—to see if I was available. I can't even remember who it was. I can't remember the face. It's a blur. I can only remember the grief of

Chapter 1

the moment when I shared my regrets and saw their shoulders slump. Now, I don't know what kind of moment it was. I don't know what I should have done. And that's just the point: *I don't know.* I had no discernment in the moment, and I have no recollection of a person I let down.

The next person's name I remember. A cancer diagnosis had hit the family hard. While still faithful, stable, and joyful, this family was also heart-weary and hand-wringing about what it would mean. I sat in their living room. "We are so glad you came. Some people told us not to ask because you wouldn't be able to visit us. Because you're just so busy." My first (frustrated) reaction was, "Who in the world told them not to ask their pastor to visit them?" My second (frustrated) reaction was, "Why in the world would they think I was too busy?" My third (humbled) reaction was: "Regardless of who said the words, I told them I was too busy. They are only relaying information that I have been living out in real time."

Better pace is not simply about being a better pastor but being a brighter person. When I'm caught in the trap of squeezing everything out of the day like a juiced orange slice with just one shred of pulp left clinging to the skin, I will kill my Sabbath. I don't mean sacrifice my Sabbath. A sacrifice is giving up something good for the sake of something better or in honor to something greater—which is why sacrificing Sabbath is an oxymoron. Sabbath is a gift from God and a way to honor God. In killing my Sabbath I wasn't giving something up as a sign of honor, trust, and gratitude; I was taking something good and wasting it in an act of horror, terror, and greed. Oh, but I'm crafty. Maybe you are, too. I wouldn't kill my Sabbath all at once. It was death by a thousand time-saving shortcuts—a bit of sermon prep; a quick pastoral text; a phone call while walking to the park with my kids; slipping into the office to print an article to get ready for a meeting. You get the idea. But what was supposed to give me a tiny edge in time management, became a jagged blade cutting bitter rips in my life. Rather than enjoying the fruit of my labor as the Teacher wrote in Ecclesiastes, I would become bitter to the unending force of my toil. Without Sabbath, I felt forced. The small, steady, simple tasks that help run a home became irritating. I don't know how many kairos moments I missed—whether in my own life, the life of my family, or the life of my church—but, thankfully, time is outside my control. If it was in my control, I would try to go back and fix my mistakes. Instead, I am learning to treat time as a gift—one given to me and one given to others—and to posture myself humbly and gratefully toward the future, believing that whatever God will give, it will be enough.

Kairos moments are about *timing*. My children are starting to develop their sense of humor. (I hope they get their mother's.) While they are memorizing content and mastering form, they still mistake *timing*. A joke can't come at any old point in the ongoing tick-tock time line; jokes often need to come at just the right time. Thankfully, the right time comes. But it comes not just for jokes, but for jumps, shifts, and changes in life, too. The kairos moment is like a hinge placed in the chronological line, a moment when life can take a new turn. As a joke at the right time can light up a room, the kairos moment is a moment in time that can alter the trajectory of a life.

Pastors are needed in the kairos moment! If you have fostered the right impressions, people will seek you out. Pay attention! Of course, it's not providential timing every time someone wants your attention. If you think every moment is filled with meaning, your calendar will be meaninglessly filled. You might be fretfully busy and frightfully stressed, but you won't be faithfully present when the timing is right. Yet with your help—including proper attention, work, and support—kairos moments can lead to meaningful change.

From Discernment to Design

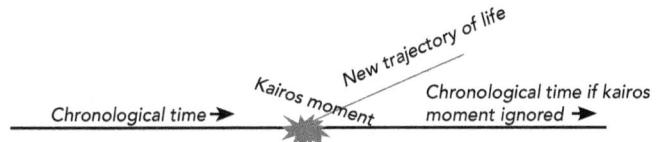

The kairos moment is to lead to a new trajectory in life. Needed in the kairos moment, properly discerned, is a *structured and supported context of change* for the person to examine her life and to be changed by the power of the Holy Spirit in the context of Christian community. Without structure and support, the trajectory of change is not likely to continue for long. This

Chapter 1

isn't about finding more willpower. Rather the support offers steps to practice a change of heart and mind, which is a process of repentance. The model helps the pastor guide the parishioner *through repentance* (which includes seeing reality, owning their own role in reality, and turning away from these patterns) and *into belief* (which includes sensing an emerging reality, owning their role in its creation, and acting in faith toward new patterns).

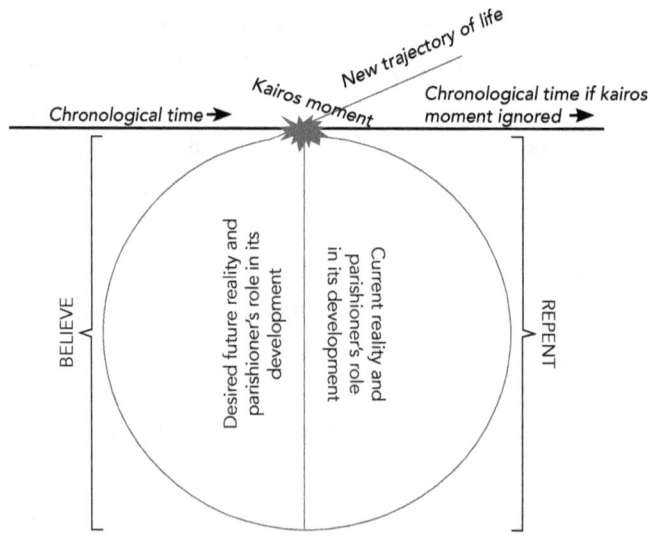

The Two Sides of the Kairos Process:
Repent and Believe

Repent

Repentance can happen in a (kairos) moment and it can also happen over time. Let's think of repentance this way. I used to live near the busiest highway in Canada, the Macdonald-Cartier Freeway, or "the Four-Oh-One" (401). Living just outside a great little city, Brockville, Ontario, my family often traveled the 401 West to a Canada–USA border entry to visit my (lovely) parents-in-law, and we also traveled east to start the journey to visit my (just as lovely) family. If we were heading west, I would wind through some back roads to the 401; but if we were heading east, I would go through Brockville. One day I happened to be in Brockville, but I needed to take 401 West. Rather than going west, my autopilot kicked in and I went *east*.

I didn't realize it right away. Having traveled the road many times, I was primed to turn by where I entered the highway, so I was unaware that I was going the opposite direction that I needed to go! Eventually, I realized my error and started to look for ways to turn around. I knew I needed to turn around, *but I could not turn around any time I wanted*. Traveling sixty-five to seventy miles per hour surrounded by traffic makes for a difficult U-turn! I started looking for an off-ramp. While I already knew I needed to turn around and my driving attention had shifted, I couldn't yet change my direction.

A change of heart and life (*metanoia* or repentance) is similar. We are going the wrong direction without knowing it until God graciously prompts us and opens our mind to a new reality and provides the time for it to take place. It's a kairos moment—God is prompting the person that something needs to change. Repentance is about changing direction. Repentance is about *turning*.

But there's a persistent challenge to turning life around. Suppose my driving error didn't happen once but kept happening over and again. Careful attention would diagnose what was contributing to this error. Life change is not immediate. It takes time and attention and patience. Repentance is also about *tuning*. Whether slightly adjusting the dial of an AM/FM radio, tightening the string of a guitar, or tweaking the mix of vocals, tuning can make a big difference. Repentance might not be about only turning from the completely wrong direction but making slight, intentional adjustments for clarity and harmony. It would mean tuning my driving attention to *avoid* taking the wrong direction. Repentance is about tuning our ears to attend clearly and carefully to God so that it is God's voice we hear and seek. My friend in the coffee shop moment didn't need a complete turnaround, but he did need *tuning* in the moment.

Whether turning or tuning, the right side of the diagram is about repenting. While the kairos moment inspires some kind of change, it requires careful attention to the complexities of life to make proper observations and interpretations. When we think of repentance as turning and tuning, then we see how it can cover a range of experiences. We should also say that sometimes the person's participation in their current reality might be more or less prominent. Some events have happened in the parishioner's life that were beyond their control. They played *no* role in their occurrence. The notion of *tuning* should encourage faith—loyalty and fidelity to God—that God is at work and the parishioner can respond to God's grace by attending to God in this moment.

Believe

The left side of the diagram is about believing. Like repentance, belief also takes time to build, practice, and strengthen. In Luke's Gospel, an angel promises Zechariah that, even though he and his wife, Elizabeth, are old, she will conceive and give birth to a son, whom they are to name John. But because Zechariah doesn't initially believe, he is unable to speak until the boy is born (Luke 1:20). An angel also appears to Mary and announces that she will be with child. Zechariah had asked the question, "How can I be sure?" (Luke 1:18 CEB), but Mary asks the question, "How will this happen?" (Luke 1:34 CEB). In contrast to Zechariah who is silenced, Mary believes and is blessed and bursts out in song (Luke 1:45-55)!

But Mary's belief seems to stall. When presenting Jesus at the temple, Simeon warns that Mary's own soul will be pierced because of Jesus's mission. Will Mary cling to her own vision for her son, or will she entrust him to God? Mary is not mentioned by name in Luke's Gospel after chapter 2, and when she is mentioned, it is in tension or opposition to Jesus. Jesus's mother and his brothers have come to see him (Luke 8:19-20) and Jesus's mother is blessed by a woman from a crowd (Luke 11:27), but in both cases, Jesus puts the focus back on hearing and obeying God and God's word (Luke 8:21; 11:28). But Mary's story is not yet finished. She reappears in the Upper Room, after the Ascension of Jesus, joining together with the disciples in prayer (Acts 1:14). Mary believed in the initial moment of the angel's announcement, and it took time for her belief to take root and bear fruit.[4]

Belief can be a process for the rest of us, too! Belief starts as a seed, graciously given, in the resolve to change heart and mind, yet it takes time for roots to grow and to bear fruit as we practice a new way of living. Belief takes root in the moment of repentance because it is God's work to alert us to our waywardness. Without God's intervention, we would not even be aware of the opportunity and need for repentance. And here's the good news: God does not stop intervening in the life of faith! God enables our repentance and belief all the way through!

I need to offer two clarifications at this point. First, these are large categories. Repentance and belief may happen in a moment, but they also happen over time. Because God is the one graciously enabling repentance and belief, they cannot be forced. Second, the parishioner may have concepts in mind that do not exactly fit what I have described above. "Repentance" might have a connotation of turning from willful sin for the parishioner, whereas their repentance is a process of turning from a life built around harm they have suffered. While there is still "repentance" happening, the pastor might not use this terminology, instead listening to pick up language that the parishioner finds helpful to describe what God is doing. (We will explore this more in depth in the chapters on listening and clarifying.)[5]

Building the Model

We now have a working theology and purpose for this model. Its theology is grounded in the incarnation and the everydayness of life into which God may break with a transformational season or moment, enabling repentance and fostering belief. It is grounded in a philosophy of structure and support to create a context of change. Both of these affirmations include the pastor. The pastor is present in the everydayness of life to help discern the moment and to help structure the context and support the parishioner through change. The pastor is a companion in the life of repentance and belief.

For the remainder of this chapter, I will sketch out the stages of the model, inserted in the diagram below, very briefly. This is a quick view at the whole before we delve more deeply into the theology, philosophy, and possible practice of each stage in the following chapters.

Chapter 1

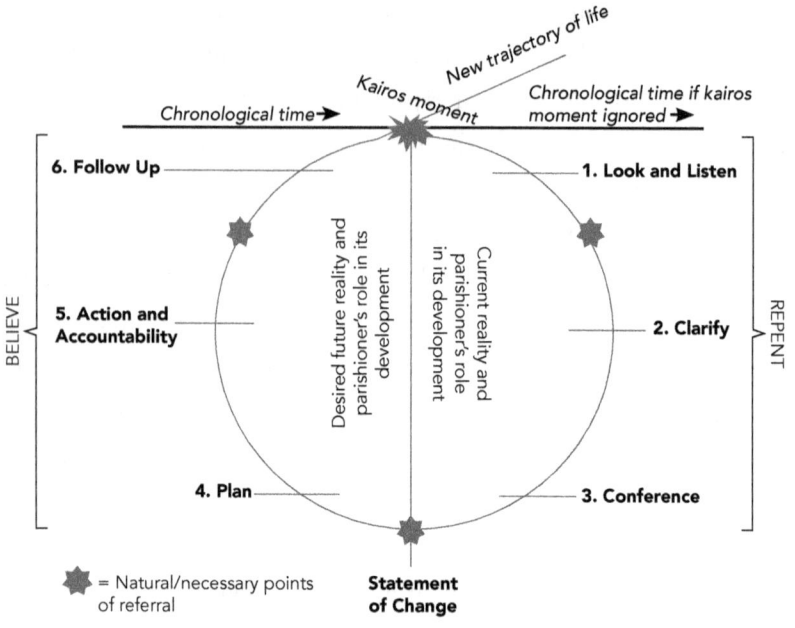

The Kairos Care Model

Step 1: Look and Listen

Listening is deceptively difficult. Because we listen every day, we think we do it well. However, if we were to receive frank and honest feedback from spouses and close friends, we will almost certainly find ways we can improve as listeners. Many of us listen very poorly—at least at certain times of the day or on certain days of the week.

Listening is not merely pausing our speech; waiting for our turn to talk; or formulating a response. Listening is a practice of empathy. Carl Rogers described empathy as "entering the private perceptual world of the other and thoroughly becoming at home in it."[6] Listening is the embodied practice of empathy.

And we listen with the body—the whole body! The movement and place of our eyes, the posture of our shoulders, and the placement of our hands can all help or hinder our listening and can all communicate our empathy (or lack thereof). We must be attuned to our own self—both internally and externally. Our bodies will also tell us if we're ready to listen. Are we physically tired? Are we distracted? Are our eyes drawn to the window or passersby? Listening is not only about using our bodies and sensing our bodies but observing the other person. We listen not only with our ears but with our eyes, as well. We observe whatever there is to be seen about the person. Is the person fidgeting, picking their fingers, slouched over, leaned in?

Listening involves taking in a whole range of information, including information that is shared intentionally, information that is shared unintentionally, and information that is shared in the moment, facilitated in the context of an active and attentive listener. In listening, we attend to the whole person, which includes what is being said verbally and what is being said physically. Are we hearing the words? Are we observing the emotion and demeanor? Is there a match between content and attitude?

This kind of personal presence is draining and difficult; it takes determination and spiritual depth. Pastors must *prepare* to listen. Pastors must *practice* listening. A well-prepared listener will elicit more from the speaker than the speaker even intended to share. A well-prepared listener will elicit more from the speaker than the speaker *thought they had to share*. Have you ever been in a pastoral counseling situation and heard something like, "I didn't think I'd tell you this, but . . ."? It's possible that the line is a manipulation technique (intentional or not); it's also possible that your intentional presence as a listener prepared a place for more to be said. Good listening welcomes more speaking.

Yet because of the time-sensitive nature of pastoral counseling, pastors can't listen indefinitely. Pastors are not simply ongoing listeners but people set aside by God to help those God brings to experience change in specific situations. Pretending we can listen with unlimited time is another way of trying to control time. Time is a gift—one to be given to one in need, but not a gift that we conjure and control so as to give it indefinitely and without limit. As a result, we should have some idea of what we are listening *for*.[7]

Chapter 1

Referral

Within this step on the diagram, there is also a star symbol, which marks the first natural point for referral. After a brief classroom discussion on the practice and ethics of referral, a hand shot into the air. "You mean we should just dump the person at the curb and run?" It was clear the questioner vocalized what several had been wondering. Let me be clear, in case that image has ever come to your mind about referral: No! Referral is not dumping the person at the curb and running! Referral is sometimes a necessary act of pastoral ministry, but it is not the end of being a pastor.

Referral may be part of the kairos moment in two ways. First, referral may be necessary because the pastor is not appropriately trained to care for the person. Ongoing or historical issues of physical pain, mental health, addiction, trauma, sexual abuse, and various forms of violence may all require professional care outside the pastoral scope of care. *God really is doing something, and the person needs to know it.* The pastor may be God's person to guide the parishioner to the right professional. Second, the kairos moment may be about handling more than one area that God is addressing. The pastor may continue working with the parishioner even while the parishioner is under the care of another professional. So referral may be in addition to providing pastoral counsel. The pastor's role is to care for the soul—the whole being in embodied relationship with God. Such care may include actions that affect and are affected by many of the issues requiring other professional care (e.g., trauma, abuse, addiction). The pastor might be helpful in shepherding a person through, for example, forgiveness (including forgiving oneself), apologizing, reconciliation, spiritual formation, and recovery even when the parishioner is being seen by a professional or specialist.

So what is referral? Referral is the act of connecting the person to another trained professional who is needed in the person's ongoing healing and care. While the pastor is trained, gifted, and given for the care of the soul, God has also provided other healers for the well-being of our people. It will take pastoral discernment at different points in the kairos model to determine whether pastoral counsel will continue or cease with referral.

If referral is necessary, here is how to be ready to avoid simply kicking a person to the curb and running. I use the acronym FRAME for Familiarize, Recommend, Accompany, Meet, Expect. Let's unpack these actions.

Familiarize: Prepare for referral by becoming familiar with a variety of professionals and services in your geographic area (or that provide appropriate online services) that fit the purpose of God to form the person to the image of Christ. This is difficult work. It is not done with a simple internet search. Just because a person is a professing Christian does not automatically mean they will implicitly support or facilitate the soul-work God desires to do. Knowing to whom you may entrust a person often takes time and personal recommendations from others. You will likely identify excellent healing professionals who practice outside the tradition of your congregation or denomination. Use your empathy skills to realize that God can and does work through healers who are formed by experiences and beliefs different than your own. Familiarity with other pastors and persons of faith in your area is very important. Familiarity with professional counselors, marriage and family therapists, psychologists, social workers, medical doctors, and lawyers in your area is vital pastoral work. It is convenient to start by becoming familiar with these professionals who are already connected or associated with your church or familiar with your pastoral care, but make sure to know their own professional preferences and boundaries. For example, I have had professional counselors who were open to serving people in the church (provided they had appropriate boundaries) and other counselors who maintained boundaries by not serving people in their local church. Even if these professionals do not provide services for people in their own local church, they may be able to recommend other trusted professionals.

Recommend: Familiarity with various professionals allows you to make appropriate recommendations. Just as some professionals may not accept clients from their church, likewise some parishioners may want to see others outside their church. The pastor's referral may come with specific recommendation when the pastor has well-founded confidence in their professional abilities and services. Over time, become more familiar with those who have been recommended to you so that your recommendation is more personal.

Accompany: Every person who comes to the pastor for support, care, and spiritual counsel is already taking a courageous step. For that person to take another courageous step to the professional the pastor has recommended may be a step too far to take on one's own. Consider what accompanying steps might be possible and appropriate to support the person. This might include anything from a text message to ask if an appointment has been made to physically accompanying a person to the appropriate office until other support can be secured from family or social services.

Meet: If a person needs other kinds of support before pastoral counsel is appropriate, then it doesn't mean the person doesn't need a pastor. In fact, the pastor may need to *increase* their activity in the person's life during this time! Rather than meeting in a structured way, the pastor may need to initiate (and be available for) more informal support. For example, rather than meeting every week in person to advance the person's godly aims and purposes, the pastor may initiate multiple phone calls or online meetings and a more informal conversation and prayer to express care, support, and encouragement. Or, rather than meeting every two weeks, the pastor may guide meeting every few days for a brief season. Referral is about clarity of what support is most needed, not necessarily about offering less time and attention. Definitely not about kicking to the curb!

Expect: Keep the faith that God is at work! The pastor provides a unique vantage point: Not only does the pastor care for the whole being, but also the pastor maintains confidence about the person's destiny, which is to be conformed to the image of Christ. Your faith will influence the faith of the parishioner. Look for ways to share your faith throughout the process of referral.

In summary, the kairos model presumes a measure of strength on behalf of the person coming to the pastor for support. The person should be capable of formulating a clear plan and taking meaningful action. What the person needs is spiritual support and guidance along the way with a pastor who is working in conjunction with the person's faith, theological beliefs, and spiritual growth. The structure of the model is to help keep pastoral counsel on task, focused, and humble. If the pastor finds that the person needs other forms of care, then referral is necessary.

Step 2: Clarify

Pastoral leadership involves four kinds of action: Observation, Interpretation, Correction, and Application.[8] If the first step is strictly about observation—listening with our whole bodies—then the second step is about observation and interpretation. We are trying to get a sense of what is happening, of why the person has come to see us. We listen and we clarify what we are hearing while we are *beginning* to make an interpretation.

It's dangerous to rush into interpretation. I used to supervise pastoral interns and residents. These soon-to-be or recent college and university graduates were learning new responsibilities and new roles. Making a shift from relatively little responsibility to managing a life and work responsibilities is quite a bit to take in all at once. Inevitably, a day would come when an intern was not at his or her best. While I had the privilege of seeing conscientious, determined, and eager emerging leaders because of my work responsibilities, not everyone in the church had the same vantage point. In a busy church with volunteers and parishioners coming and going, parishioners would sometimes see these young leaders at less than their best. Even the most competent couldn't show their best self all the time. When this day would come, we would discuss the importance of self-presentation. The point of the feedback: "Don't give people a good reason to make a bad interpretation of who you are."

We all make interpretations without even knowing it. In the clarification step, pastors must work at withholding final interpretations because these will be bad interpretations—even if they have (initial) good reasons. Pastors must check assumptions and test initial hypotheses. By clarifying one's observations and going slow with interpretation, pastors can widen the knowledge base from which they will eventually make informed interpretations. By becoming familiar with and then applying different psychological theories of the human person, interpretations can be improved, and the interpretation process strengthened. Pastors can develop a kind of mental checklist—a way to see beneath the surface so that our superficial understanding doesn't unnecessarily box us in. Remember, these kinds of conversations can happen on the fly, so a working knowledge of a few tools is important.

Chapter 1

Step 3: Conference

Pastors must *relate* to other people. Meaningful relationships are always reciprocal. While professional counselors must be mindful of and usually avoid dual relationships—having more than one way of relating to the client (for example, when a counselor offers professional counseling to a cousin, investment partner, physician, etc.)—pastors are almost always in dual relationships with people. A pastor is possibly a friend of the parishioner; together they are part of God's family. The pastor might be in the same small group or work side by side in a ministry with the person seeking counsel. The pastor might serve on a board, either inside the church or outside the church, with a parishioner. You get the idea. Dual relationships happen. In fact, the pastor is often sought out *because* of this other relationship. In other contexts, pastors have shown themselves to be thoughtful, informed, and professional. People believe pastors can care for their whole self.

So how should pastors handle dual relationships? Pastors must relate carefully because relationships are reciprocal. They go both ways. Any one-way engagement is not a relationship. It's a kind of service. Reciprocity, however, involves appropriate disclosure. Pastors must learn to let others in on their personal story and authentic self appropriately, but without turning the tables, without comparing pain and becoming the one cared for by the parishioner in this moment. Developing this authentic persona takes some coaching and training.

In the conferencing step, pastors are working with the parishioner to make a good interpretation of what is going on. This is collaborative work. It's not about the pastor convincing the parishioner about what the problem is or announcing the discovery of the parishioner's otherwise hidden problems. Pastoral counsel, instead, involves working with the other through open-ended questions with tentative offers of the pastor's insights to come to a good interpretation.

Interlude: Statement of Change

The work of the first three steps should culminate in a clear understanding of what the parishioner wants to see happen through God's transforming grace. Let's call this the "Statement of Change." This statement should give clarity both to the pastor and to the parishioner so that one of two things can happen. Either there is a clear agreement about where these conversations ought to lead, or there is clarity that the pastor does not support or is not well-equipped to support the desired change. Sometimes a parishioner may have desires that the pastor might not agree with. The pastor may even believe these desires to be harmful to the parishioner or to others. However, when the Statement of Change is clear and commendable, then there can be a clear course of action. For example, in my coffee shop conversation, when my friend decided to start his own business, we didn't circle back as to whether or not this was the right choice. It was clear what he wanted, and it was a choice I could support. So we discussed how best to handle announcing this decision—timing, procedure of informing his close relationships, professional obligations, and so on. The desired future was clear, and a way forward was possible.

However, I have also been in conversations in which parishioners wanted futures that I didn't support or couldn't help them to bring about while maintaining my convictions and conscience. These scenarios included pursuing unhealthy relationships or attending to passions that would disorder the person's life. Sometimes the pastor may need more time to reflect or more information and context to support the choice. At other times, the pastor will encourage the parishioner to delay making a choice to get a longer-term perspective from the current moment. If the pastor cannot support the Statement of Change, either because of its nature or its timing, there is a shift to step 6 (Follow Up). The pastor does not cut off the relationship but figures out how to navigate the relationship as the pastor. The person may need professional help that the pastor can't provide, but the pastor is still to provide spiritual care. Or, while not supporting the person's desired future, the pastor will remain the pastor and, hopefully, a redemptive person in the parishioner's life.

Step 4: Plan

Every statement of change involves a goal. Goals are more often accomplished with plans—broad strategies and specific action steps that are laid out and considered against alternatives. The kairos moment is about achieving some kind of change. Pastoral counseling always includes the intention of getting somewhere. It involves seeing something coming to be that is not yet.

Good news! Pastors often thrive at goal setting! Many are trained in developing goals, reverse engineering, and strategic planning. Challenging news: The pastor is not in the charge of the other; it is not the *pastor's* goal to achieve. While the pastor brings a plethora of skills to this step—and if not, then we've included some in the corresponding chapter—pastors must be careful to maintain what is called *differentiation*. Differentiation means that the pastor is separate from the parishioner and maintains a sense of self that is, to a great degree, insulated from the parishioner's choices, even as the pastor is tempted to become more invested.

Step 5: Action and Accountability

Up to now, pastors have acted: they have listened, clarified, conferenced, planned, and so on. They have not done this work in isolation, of course, but now they must take a different posture. In step 5, pastors, even while playing this part all along, more clearly become cheerleaders and coaches. Pastors can't implement the plan; only the parishioners can do so. Yet pastors can provide support along the way—encouragement, cheering, and affirmation. They can also provide accountability by asking questions, digging into details, and finding out what's going on outside the pastoral counseling conversation. Did their parishioners do what they said they would do? Did they take action in the form that was decided upon? Do they need more specific action steps? Are smaller steps needed? Are they giving a good faith effort or just going through the motions or something in between? What problems emerged that need to be solved?

My father was a teacher. He liked teachers. He hung around teachers. One teaching colleague went on to become a very successful coach in the National Hockey League. As two people who grow up alongside one another in small towns often know, while one might achieve a measure of fame and success, when you know each other from days spent together in school, cafeterias, hockey rinks, softball diamonds, and the everydayness of life, there remains a mutual humility. With just a few tweaks, one life could have turned out like the other. Though lives were led differently, these friends can still learn from each other. The coach, one of the most respected men in the game, shared a bit of wisdom that he knew my father, as a teacher, already knew: "Ellard, the key is knowing which player needs accountability and motivation and which player needs comfort and encouragement."

Pastors: Even in holding the other to account, bear in mind mutuality and cooperation. Know whether *you* prefer to give accountability and motivation or comfort and encouragement. Also, work at discerning what *the parishioner* might need and how *they* might respond. Sometimes it can be trial and error. In all this, never forget that while someone is coming to you for counsel, life could have taken (and perhaps yet will take) a radical turn. That person could be in your seat and you in that person's seat. There is a mutual humility even while there is a seriousness of calling and role as the other takes specific actions to see effective change.

Finally, this is another natural point of referral. Sometimes two skilled, motivated, and faithful people just aren't successful at achieving certain change. It's not the time to give up, but to document all that has been tried and to bring another person into the conversation who might be effective at helping the parishioner see the change come about. Pastors: While it might be humbling to admit this state of affairs, you will need to remain a cheerleader because the parishioner knows they will need to work up the courage and perseverance to go through a version of this process with someone else.

Step 6: Follow Up

The final step is navigating the ongoing pastoral relationship once pastoral counseling has been completed. Like I said above, people come to pastors *because* they already have a relationship. But some people might delay coming to the pastor because they don't want this relationship to change. They need to overcome a certain amount of fear—fear of being judged, fear of being labeled, fear of becoming a project, fear of being ignored. Coming to the pastor risks the whole relationship. So relationship is what prompts going to see the pastor, and relationship is what delays the choice, as well. What a tension!

If the conversation or set of conversations has progressed right through to Follow Up, then these fears may start to reemerge. On the one hand, the relationship has likely deepened—the pastor has shared part of their own journey and been invited into a meaningful and important time in the other's life. There have been successes and failures and transformations—all of which the pastor has seen from a unique vantage point. On the other hand, this unique relationship is coming to an end. Scheduled and structured meetings, homework, and debriefing are no longer necessary. It is a very real concern: What form will the relationship take?

Pastors can alleviate some of this anxiety both for themselves and for the parishioner by being proactive and communicative and having a plan. I have seen completed pastoral counseling lead to renewed faith, greater service within the church, and amplified leadership by the parishioner. I have also seen completed pastoral counseling lead to seeking a new church (or no church, for a season or even longer). Take note: *Seeking a new church was not the result of ineffective pastoral counsel.* It was sometimes the result of a failure in Follow Up. Follow Up was left alone, simply ignored. Somebody thought things would "go back to normal."

But normal is precisely what the kairos moment wants to change! If things *don't* go back to normal, then something has been achieved! The new pastor-parishioner relationship needs to recognize this change and account for it as a new relationship is navigated. Wisdom and clarity in step 6 can save a whole lot of hurt, but it is so easy to forget. Don't forget it! I will introduce some techniques and further rationale later in the book.

Drawing the Model

We have now gone through the entire model. We can picture it like this. I have inserted the broader categories of Observe, Interpret, Correct, and Apply to show where they overlap with the six steps.

The Model

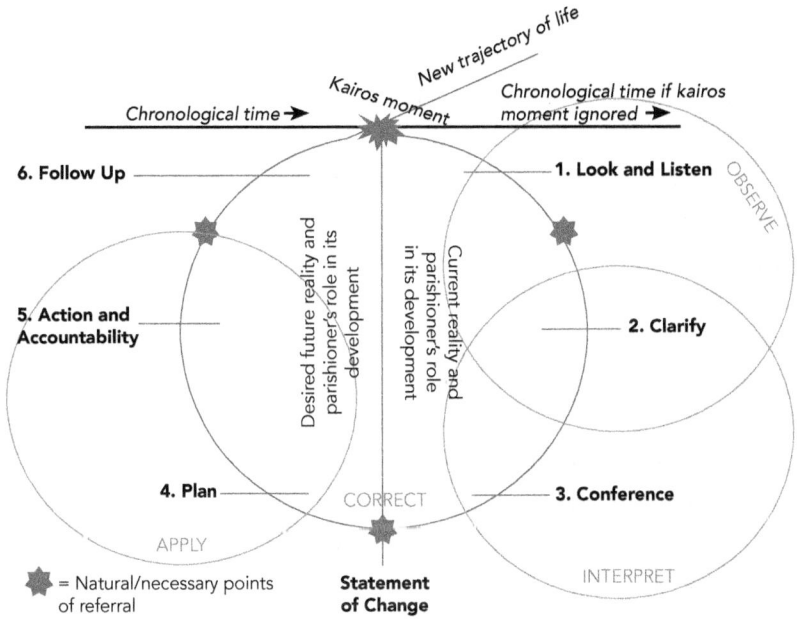

Take a look at the diagram. Think through it. Now set the book aside, and try to draw it out from memory on a physical piece of paper. Don't worry about getting every detail.

I'll wait.

No rush. Well, maybe a little.

Now, compare your diagram with the one I've presented above. How did you do? It might be the case that where the diagram flowed easily is what you already do naturally and with a measure of skill, but that where you struggled is a step you don't naturally do. Pay attention to your own diagram; it might be the start of your personalized model.

If you find that a kairos model is a valuable tool, then I strongly suggest drawing out the model for the parishioner. Now, this might not happen in the first session or two, but if a strategic set of meetings looks like it will be a good idea, I suggest taking the time to map out the model so that the parishioner knows the process that will be taken. Once you reach the Follow Up stage, there will already be some mutual understanding.

Chapter 1

"This Isn't That Hard"

I was sitting in a room of denominational leaders, listening to a relational expert talk about the recovery of pastors who had suffered some kind of crisis or failure. The process he had developed to help pastors move on from failure or breakdown included transitioning pastors and their families to supportive churches who would nurture them back into a Christian community and fruitful living, while helping them find employment and a small social network. This impressive ministry didn't always mean the restoration of the man or woman into pastoral ministry (or restoring one's family), but it was evident that this was life-changing work. We were all impressed. And then the expert let us in on the secret. He lowered his voice, moving from an excited, powerful teaching voice to a gentle, encouraging voice: "This isn't that hard." He didn't mean that the life change wasn't *challenging*; the accountability, the network, the listening, the on-the-ground ministry happening for these pastors and their families is emotional work. He meant that it wasn't overly complex. It took effort, authenticity, and guts.

Wow! What a word! The work was vital, life-changing, necessary, and available—*"and not that hard."* I have learned to see pastoral counseling in a similar vein. Pastoral counseling is vital and necessary; it can be life changing; I am sure someone in your church needs to avail themselves of it yesterday. But in the end, pastoral counseling—whether a one-on-one conversation in a coffee shop or a series of conversations in the home or office—*isn't about complexity, but work, wisdom, and will.*

Chapter 2

Look and Listen

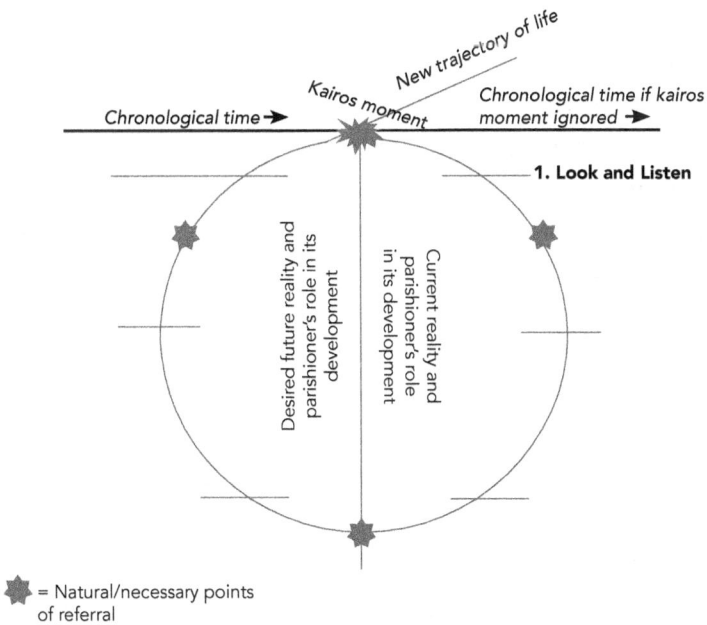

Listening Is Harder Than We Think

What does it mean to listen? There is more than one way to think about listening.[1] Think about the last time that *you* felt really listened to. What was it like? Most likely the listener was emotionally present, physically engaged, and able to understand what you shared.[2] Listening is a tremendous gift. Listening tangibly communicates the personal value of the speaker. A good listener shows the speaker that they are worth the emotional cost through physical posture and intellectual effort. There is power and potential in the first step of the pastoral conversation and counsel. We listen every day. At least we try to. But we dare not assume we do this well. And we risk missing vital theology for listening if we skip over the first step. In this chapter, I will offer a brief theology of listening, point out some barriers to listening, and then offer simple listening techniques.

The Whole Truth

Jesus models this kind of emotional, physical, intellectual listening in Mark 5:21-43. Jairus, a synagogue ruler, has pleaded earnestly for Jesus to come to his home and heal his daughter; but before Jesus is able to depart, a woman with a chronic bleeding condition reaches out to touch him. Jesus has stopped the journey to Jairus's home to find out who has touched him. The disciples protest, perhaps because it's a futile effort or because a synagogue ruler is a prominent person, but Jesus insists: Who touched him?

Consider the courageous offender, a woman who has been bleeding for twelve years. What aspect of her suffering would have been worse: Having a chronic bleeding condition that would have kept her ceremonially unclean (Lev 12:15) for twelve years? Or would it have been worse to suffer the consistent failure of the medical community? We don't know the abilities or intentions of the doctors she saw, but we do know she spent all her money (Mark 5:26). We can imagine the inner strength she would have stirred up for each visit, each fresh attempt to be well. If you have ever been in chronic pain or been treated consistently as an outsider, then you can easily put yourself in the position of this woman. After touching Jesus's clothes and knowing she is healed, she is called out in front of everyone. "The woman, full of fear and trembling, came forward. Knowing what had happened to her, she fell down in front of Jesus and told him the whole truth" (Mark 5:33 CEB).

How long do you think it took to tell Jesus *the whole truth*? To tell Jesus about twelve years of suffering, of financial loss, of exclusion? Would this story take thirty minutes? An hour? Two hours? We don't know. Mark leaves it open-ended, and our imaginations are engaged. Now imagine Jairus and his entourage standing and waiting for this encounter to end. But there is Jesus—engaged and conversing with the woman, modeling the full extent of her healing as someone listens to her in a most meaningful way, perhaps for the first time in twelve years. He is emotionally present, physically engaged, and intellectually interested and capable.

In this narrative, Jesus shows us how to listen. To explore what this story means, we'll consider a theological framework, which is modified for the purposes of pastoral conversation.

Putting Jesus in the Middle

In addition to the liturgical purpose of the creation story, which culminates on a Sabbath day of rest for praising God, one of the aims of the Genesis creation stories is to situate humankind, to give a context for what it means to be human. There are four large contexts to consider: First, God is the overarching context. In the beginning, God created the heavens and the earth (Gen 1:1), and the Lord God made the earth and the heavens (Gen 2:4). The first creation story presents the challenge right away: the earth is formless and empty (Gen 1:2) and God's solution unfolds systematically. On days one to three, God *forms* space and structure, and on days four to six, God *fills* the space. The order is seen clearly as the days correspond, day one to day four, day two to day five, and day three to day six. Human beings find their place in the story on day six. God's unfolding creation saga produces a human being capable of *filling* the earth, just as God had filled the space God formed.

The second creation story presents the challenge after a little bit. The man has already been given a place (2:8), a purpose (2:15), and provision (2:16). But what he lacks is companionship. Among all the other animals, none is a suitable helper for the man's mission (2:20). So once again God creates—the

Chapter 2

woman. The story anticipates the male and female filling the earth through the fruitfulness of their relationship.

So God acts to form, fill, and make the creation fruitful. The creation involves the fertile land, the soil from which our food will come and out of which the man was formed. It also involves the animals, including the land animals, which, like the human beings, were also created on the sixth day. It also involves other human beings. Male and female naturally lead to fruitfulness and other human beings. Finally, there is a context of the self. When the man named all the animals, he realized that he was different from all of them; when the man saw the woman, he realized that while she was distinct from the man, she was also like the man.

"God saw how good it was" (Gen 1:31). "The man and his wife were naked, and they felt no shame" (Gen 2:25). The two phrases—one repeated through the first six days of creation and the second phrase the summary of the second creation narrative—indicate a pristine harmony found across the beautiful creation and its multiple relationships. God is in relationship with the entire creation, especially through the man and woman in relationship with each other and the creation, including the fertile land and animals.

Let's put these contexts and relationships in a diagram.

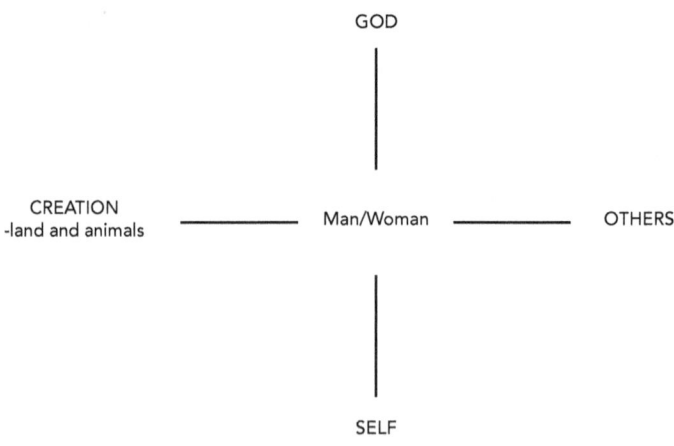

Four Contexts of Creation in Harmony

This comprehensive harmony, pulsing with loyal love, is what God intends, but, of course, the Genesis story soon shows the breakdown of every context. The human beings, rather than preserving and sustaining their fidelity in an Edenic garden, allow it to be defiled. The woman and man mutually fail each other as the woman and man give in to their selfish desires (3:6). The fruit of the tree doesn't give life but leads to death. The fruit of the ground will come through painful toil and anxiety (3:17-19), and the fruitfulness of humankind will be marked with pain (3:16). The man names the woman, taking a dominating role (3:20), and the woman's desire for her husband will mean abdicating to his unhealthy rule (3:16). The man and the woman are now aware of themselves and hide from God (3:10).

Parents of adolescent children often notice their attempts to hide. I can remember the first time my daughter had a sense of self-awareness. She was not being shamed in the moment, but she had an experience that would make shame possible. I can remember the shift in her eyes and face. At the moment, I could take her into my arms and quickly comfort her, assuring her of her deep and unchanging value. As she gets older, it's tougher to do so. She is taller, quicker, and more elusive—emotionally and physically. I can't take her in my arms so easily; I can't catch her so deftly; I do not always see the shift in her eyes. She can hide. As we get older, we get better at hiding. Pastors might observe this behavior sometimes with people who have resisted embrace (physical or emotional), run from relationships, and harbor hidden hurts.

The creation diagram starts to look like this:

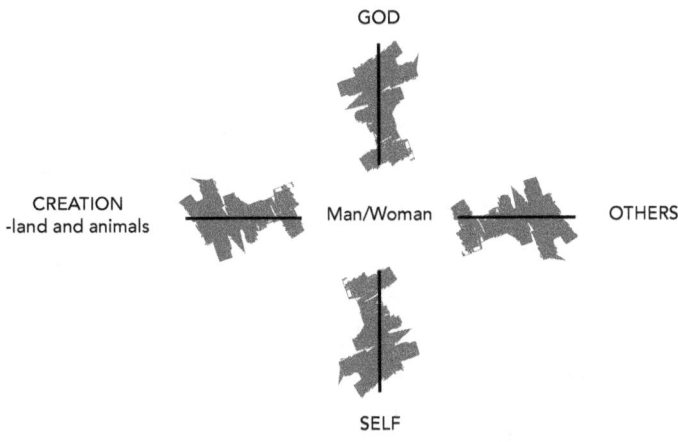

Four Contexts of Creation with Disharmony

Chapter 2

Much more could be said about these breakdowns, but let's cut to the chase. Just as God addressed the challenge of formlessness and emptiness in Genesis 1, and just as God addressed the challenge of the human's aloneness in Genesis 2, God will once again address the disharmony. Only this time, God does it not by creating from a shapeless void but by entering the creation through a woman. God the Son, in the fully human person of Jesus, comes to restore all things to perfect harmony. Jesus restores this relational harmony between God and human beings through the faithfulness of suffering death on a cross, and by entrusting himself to God and God's vindicating judgment.

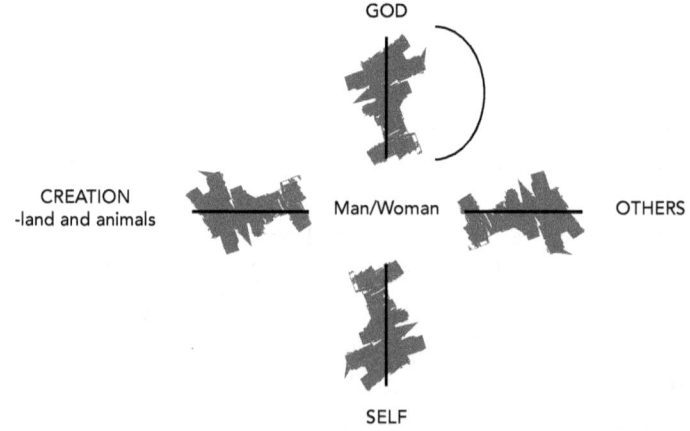

God Entering the Disharmony in Jesus

Where the man and woman succumbed to their selfish desires, Jesus renews the creation through the cross and reconciles the whole world into a right relationship. Rather than hiding from God in the garden (Gen 3:8), God's Son allows himself to be found by a gang of officials, religious leaders, and soldiers, guided by a betrayer (John 18:1-3). Rather than offering more animal skins for sacrificial coverings, Jesus exposes his own back for the covering of humankind. Whereas the man would grow food by the sweat of his brow until he returned to the ground (Gen 3:19), Jesus's bloody drops of sweat fell to the ground (Luke 22:44) before he would be crucified and buried. Rather than blaming the woman for her failure (Gen 3:12), Jesus would make sure his mother was cared for after his death (John 19:25-27). Instead of seeking status and life outside the will and timing of God, Jesus entrusts his life into the Father's hands. And, glory to God, rather than being caught in the cycle of death that humankind has always known, *you and I* can be found in Christ, and in Christ we are hidden in God (Col 3:3), under no shameful condemnation (Rom 8:1), restored and renewed in the people of God. In Christ we anticipate a full restoration of all creation (Rom 8:20-21). In other words, in Christ we are restored to God, to ourselves, to others, and we retake the truly human position to lead in creation. My own name is inserted in the diagram below, but feel free to scratch mine out and write yours in.

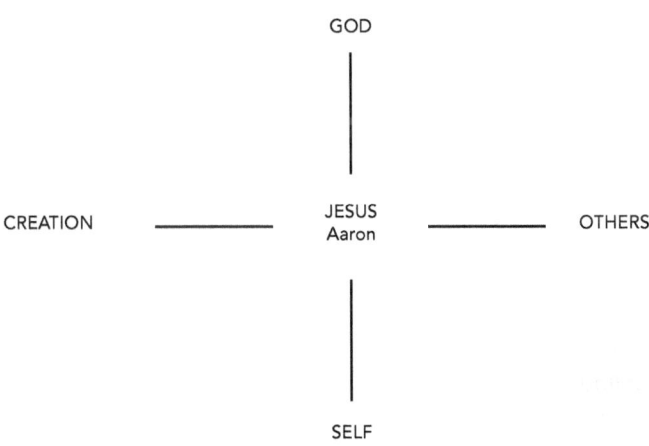

Being in Christ in the Context of Creation

So what does this have to do with listening? *Everything.* God has always been listening. Whereas the man and woman hid when they *heard* God in the garden, God acted to save God's people when he *heard them* crying out about oppression in Egypt (Exod 3:7). The Israelites' bonds were loosened because God *listened*.[3] And God continued to act by listening, most deeply, on the cross. On the cross, Jesus most radically is put into the disharmony and rupture of the creation. Jesus knows the shame of nakedness and public humiliation. The wood of the cross is the hard surface into which his wrists and ankles are nailed. There is no shame or alienation that is not experienced on the cross, and so all bonds on the soul are loosened in this great act. Just as God heard the Israelites and set them free, so Christ's cross is the place where Christ hears all the brokenness of humanity, whether the audible wailing of the mourner, scoffing of the scoundrels, jeering of the jaded, or the spiritual groaning of every alienated soul.[4]

But Jesus is not alienated from himself as he lives in perfect faithfulness to his Father and, thereby, to his own nature and character. Jesus does not go to the cross unwillingly, forced by the strength of systemic injustice. He goes because of his devotion to the Father and thereby wins the victory of the life of complete faith. It is the very nature of God to listen, even unto death.

Jesus is the model and means of listening. Let's return to the woman who had been bleeding for twelve years. Jesus puts himself into her life, refusing to allow the one who received healing simply to slip back into the crowd. Jesus is the model for listening by engaging the woman and listening to the *whole truth*. He even listens so intently with Jairus waiting—patiently or not, we don't know! With Jesus as our teacher, we are called to listen, to attend to the people who have received healing from Christ.

But we can't do this on our own. As church leaders, if it were not for God's prevenient grace at work in human lives, and if we didn't have Jesus's commandment to love our neighbor, we would be hiding and scuttling among domination, abdication, and anxiety in our relationships. But the grace of God in Christ transforms us. Christ is our means of listening. Jesus is present in these conversations by his Spirit. How different to think that we listen through Christ's prevenient presence rather than because of his absence!

Barriers to Listening

What does listening with Christ look like? Place yourself as one of the disciples in Mark 5, with the woman who was bleeding for twelve years. What would keep *you* from listening to her? If you were there, why might you have wanted to move Jesus along to Jairus's home? When we remember that listening with the heart of Christ is foreshadowing the passion of Christ, we realize why listening might be so difficult, but we also can learn to do this difficult work. Five barriers to listening are described through the acronym CHAOS: Chaotic Content, Hurry, Attitude, Offense, Scarcity.

C – Chaotic Content

Would the woman have been able to tell the whole truth in a smooth manner? Could the testimony of twelve years of suffering have flowed without repetition, clarifications, and rabbit trails? Not likely. The content would have felt chaotic. Something similar happens in the pastor's office or during pastoral conversation. Professional communications—from thirty-second advertisements to three-hour movies—focus on having a theme, a thread that unites the content. We are trained not only to *appreciate* consistency and coherence but also to *expect* it. But the speaker is not coming to the listener with a coherent story. (If the speaker has a coherent, even rehearsed story, take note! It might be a sign of seeking your affirmation, whether appropriate or not.) The speaker is often seeking out a listener *because* their story feels chaotic.

There's another way to think of chaos. A number of years ago, I was invited into a family's critical situation, which unexpectedly ended in a young man's death. The young man had gone into the hospital for what was supposed to be a routine surgery but was found to have a significant infection. He had been speaking with his mother forty-eight hours earlier; when I arrived, he was comatose, breathing only with a ventilator. I listened to his mother, a strong and faithful woman, now faced with a chaotic situation. It was a story without a reasonable ending in sight.[5] There were no answers to her questions. She knew there were no answers, but she needed to vocalize the questions, just for someone to hear them. The questions pertained not only to her son but also to her own story. If her son died, who would care for the grandchild? What was her responsibility? As I stood there, I realized that it could have been me lying in the bed; that just as this man's life had derailed so unexpectedly, so could mine.

Pastors listen to many stories without meaningful endings or turning points—loss of job, breakdown in marriage, undiagnosed illness. They could all become true in the pastor's life. Emotional disengagement, a rigid body, and lack of focus can all be signs that we are not truly listening. It is natural to protect ourselves from chaos, to refuse to entertain that our lives are as fragile as those seeking our care. But here the cross of Christ can be a pastor's resource. On the cross, Christ, too, faced the chaos of death. On the cross, Christ brings meaning to the meaningless. The senseless death of the innocent Jesus becomes the means of God's salvation—a mystery revealed and prophecies fulfilled! But keep this theological perspective about suffering in the context of listening: We do not present the cross as an answer to the one telling their story; rather we remember the cross as our internal resource while listening, knowing that the pastor is facing the chaos of the human condition as Christ's representative, not alone but as a listener in Christ! The story may not resolve in a meaningful way in the short- or medium-term; our own lives hang from many unseen threads. Yet our lives are hidden with Christ in God.

H – Hurry

How long would it take the woman to tell the whole truth? How would Jairus have been feeling? Might he have been moving Jesus along, wishing the woman would get to the point? We can't listen in a hurry. It's impossible. There are a few reasons we try to listen in a hurry.

We listen in a hurry because we are being asked to listen at an inconvenient time. Pastors are asked to listen five minutes before the service starts and fifty-five minutes after it has ended. Sometimes the inconvenience needs to be acknowledged and an appointment scheduled. In such cases, pastors can act with humility and acknowledge that they are not able to listen well in the moment but would like to schedule a time when they can listen well. I have often found that people who needed my pastoral attention were motivated to follow up with a text, phone call, or email later that day to set up an appointment. I knew I would be tempted to listen in a hurry, but since I couldn't do so, I asked the parishioner to follow up with me.

We listen in a hurry as a kind of anesthetic. Just as moving at a rapid pace through life keeps us from feeling certain pains, so does listening in a hurry keep us from encountering the deep pain of the other person. Every conversation carries a risk, a possible burden on our lives. We might be in an actual hurry, stressed by the momentary details of our calendar, or we might be a hurried person, stressed by our character.

My daughter Emma Beth loves to tell stories. When I'm trying to sort out a sibling scuffle, it's a bit of a pain. She can spin details, delay the point, and distract the parent (i.e., me). But much of the time, she just wants to tell a story. It doesn't always have a point. It's doesn't always have a theme. She's learning how to tell stories by telling stories in the presence of a listener. I recall one time that the story seemed to meander a bit more than usual. "Get to the point." The words were out of my mouth faster than I could stuff them back in. I wish she wasn't listening, but she was. She heard my curt words; she saw my hurried heart. None of us are at our listening best all the time. There are times I want to listen in a hurry. But I can't. I need to acknowledge the limit and work at a slower pace.

A – Attitude

How might the onlookers have compared the woman and Jairus? Certainly the synagogue ruler had more social standing than the woman. He was more prominent and had more social cache. One of the barriers to listening to her story might have been seeing her as a "less-than"—a person whose importance in the early movement of Jesus was much less compared to that of a synagogue ruler.

Watch out for inappropriate attitudes in listening. One selfish attitude might be that a person is not important to our work responsibilities and ministry purposes. In his letter to Miss March, John Wesley encouraged this woman of means who was going deeper in faith through the Methodist movement to visit "the poor, the widow, the sick, the fatherless." There might be no other reason "but that they are bought with the blood of Christ."[6] We must always remember that those who have no immediate value to our plans are valuable to God.

When we don't listen to those who might not fit our purposes, we shrink our experiential knowledge. In his sermon "On Visiting the Sick," John Wesley writes, "One [large] reason why the rich, in general, have so little sympathy for the poor, is, because they so seldom visit them." As a result, "one part of the world does not know what the other [part of the world] suffers."[7]

While Wesley wrote these words well over two hundred years ago, they still convict me. The other before us is a dearly loved person for whom Christ died. If I can't see them as valuable and worthy, then it is my unseeing eyes, not their deficiency.

Another attitude might be to exalt the pastoral office falsely. There needs to be discretion about the pastor's time and office. Again, the pastor is not always available. However, this discretion is because of our *limits*, not because of our *status*. After all, if Jesus has given access to the throne room of God, then Jesus has certainly given access to the pastor's office! When we recognize our limits, then we can work to address them systematically and structurally by selecting, training, and equipping others to develop their own listening skills—to join Christ in caring for others and reducing human suffering. The fruit of listening should ultimately be *more listeners*.

O – Offense

The bleeding woman had been failed. No doubt she had built up some offenses. She had used resources on physicians who couldn't help her. Is it possible that in sharing the whole truth she spoke a cutting comment, an offensive word? Sometimes our own people can offer snarky remarks. Offenses can be barriers to listening. Our previous hurts, harms, and unhealed wounds leave us exposed to the offensive words and stories we will hear. If we are deeply listening, we will hear racist, sexist, selfish words. We will hear stories of people suffering and committing shocking acts. Some of these stories will be offensive to us or remind us of offenses we have suffered or even committed. Offense can be a barrier to listening.

Deep enough beneath the surface in every heart and life—our lives included—is a wound or offense that points to the judgment that was nailed to the cross. We face judgment by continuing to sin. But we take heart: Christ is not horrified. Christ is never afraid, ashamed, or shocked. Christ has seen into the very depths of hell and was raised, his wounds healed.

Offense can be a barrier to listening. We must listen with Christ in order not to be offended, and we must be healed in Christ in order to keep our own wounds from reopening in the listening work.

S – Scarcity

Finally, scarcity is a barrier to listening. We have already addressed this in terms of the hurried life, but other forms of scarcity keep us from listening. If there is not enough time, training, and emotional bandwidth for the tasks God has given me, then something is wrong. I may be trying to do more than is asked of me. I may not have learned how to access the sufficient resources of God in Christ through the means of grace. God has provided enough for the tasks he has given us to do; he has given all we need for life and godliness (2 Pet 1:3).

Helps in Listening

There are many resources on how to listen. Here is a summary of practical application tools with the acronym LISTEN.

L – Look

Communicate your attention to the speaker with appropriate eye contact and bodily engagement. Some people may want more and some people may want less eye contact. No two speakers are exactly the same. You can also communicate your attention by being mindful of your own body's movement. Do you fidget, bounce a foot, lose attention out the window? If you need something to occupy your hands, try taking notes. Explain that you are taking notes in order to get the person's approval.

I – Invest in Conversation

Keep in mind that while this is the first step, it will (possibly) become a wider conversation. Invest in the conversation with nonverbal cues that communicate you are still listening. One way to do so is to look for and listen to small, perhaps immediately insignificant details. Richard Foster once said to look for God at work in the small corners of life. The listener can communicate interest and invest in the conversation by asking about the small corners of the story.

Invest in the conversation by asking open-ended questions—questions that aren't answered simply by *yes* or *no*. Some easy phrases to master for this skill are, "Tell me about . . ." or "What else might you say about . . ." Think about going into the person's experiences, desires, wishes. You can also offer alternatives and see which is picked up on. "Was it more like _____ or like _____?" The speaker may allow you to take a more prominent role in the conversation here, but hold off on saying too much at this point. This is about listening.

Curiosity is a tremendous aid at this point. Every story being shared with you is a testimony in the making; God is already at work! While God's work is unfolding, it can already be interesting to those with ears to hear. To be honest, it is not always easy to invest in a conversation. But, remember that you are listening with Christ. Jesus is the face you are presenting to the person, and he is the one into whose image you are being developed! When you work to show the interest of Christ, even if it is work, it is an authentic display of the true pastor.

S – Set Aside Solutions

When engaging narratives, there are two kinds of people in the world: fixers and sharers. The sharers want to share, and the fixers want to fix. It took me a while to learn that, when my wife had something she wanted me to know, she wasn't automatically asking me to fix it. Whether it was with your spouse, friend, leader, or follower, perhaps you learned this lesson quicker than me!

In the listening phase, set aside solutions. If you are taking notes, you might draw a specific column with tentative action steps. Keep these to yourself for the moment, perhaps seeing if they are helpful in the Conference or Plan steps.

T – Turn Off Technology

When listening, turn off the technology: lower your laptop and silence your cell phone. If you are taking notes on a screen, make sure that the back of the screen is not always turned toward the speaker. The speaker doesn't know what's on the screen and it's easy to wonder what another person is looking at or if that person is praying attention. I suggest taking notes on paper. Note taking with pen and paper rather than with a laptop or tablet can help with listening. If you need to use your phone to check the time, inform the person what you are doing. Keep in mind that quickly answering a text message is no different than saying, "Excuse me for a moment, I need to speak to this other person." Now, you might need to do so, but if you need to, then make sure to excuse yourself politely.

E — Empathize through Christ

It's helpful to think of empathy as being *in* the story of the other person. Just as Christ entered the story of creation as a human being, so we are able to enter the story of each other through Christ. Christ is already in the story of the other person, so if we are in Christ, we have resources to be "in" the story of another person. We can feel what they feel and identify with their perspective without forsaking convictions. We are with the other as we are in Christ who is in them.

N – Nonverbal Cues

Finally, watch for nonverbal cues. Just as your listening attention is communicated bodily, so is the speaker communicating nonverbally. This might include being distracted, speaking at a more rapid pace at times, ignoring certain questions, interrupting questions, unfocused eye contact, and other cues. Some cues might simply be physiological. The speaker might feel too warm and uncomfortable taking off their coat. The speaker might be sitting next to a draft or might need to use the washroom. Being attentive to nonverbal cues can solve relatively minor issues that can easily derail a conversation.

Post-Listening Practices

Once the listening session is over, set aside about ten to fifteen minutes to gather your thoughts, record some notes, pray, and see if any potential action is needed. If this conversation has been impromptu, it is all the more important to pause before re-entering the prior rhythm of life. It will be tempting to wrap up this time of care and to rush into something else, but hurry still isn't your ally. Give yourself some time to decompress from the difficult, pressure-filled work you've just completed. In order to guard this time, you might need to rearrange your scheduling practices. We often schedule meetings at the top of the hour, but if a previous meeting goes right down to the bottom of the hour, there's no margin. You might consider scheduling meetings to end fifteen minutes before the hour or to start fifteen minutes after the hour. If time simply isn't immediately available, then schedule it for later in the day and trust the Lord to preserve in your memory what needs to be recorded.

Gather Thoughts and Record Notes

If you haven't recorded notes as you've listened, then you will need to do some remembering. Be humble in what you remember. Rather than trying to document in detail, recall senses and impressions and use these to drive your notes. If you have done some recording as you were listening, then you will do some synthesizing—bringing together events or details under larger themes or topics. Consider the following headings: Key Words, Key People, Key Places, Key Events. A few minutes spent charting out this information will be helpful if the person returns after a couple of weeks or even longer.

Pray

You have listened with Christ, and now you are entrusting the person to Christ's love and healing. Listening is draining, but the person has now re-entered everyday life. What was draining to you might have been so very refreshing to that person. Pray for the speaker! Hold this dearly loved person before our Lord for a few moments, not only for divine support, but also to remember that Christ bears the pastor's burdens.

Plan Appropriate Action

What have you heard from the other person and from our Lord in prayer? Do you need to take a specific action? I recall one distressed phone call I received. I took time to listen and pray. I thought things were well at the end of the conversation. Or, at least, they were well enough. After hanging up the phone and taking some time to pray, I knew that an immediate in-person visit would be necessary. And it was. The telephone had provided enough distance to keep the person from disclosing their full need. This person was in distress and needed immediate help.

At least some—if not most—of the time, no further action is needed on your part except to remain appropriately available. It is often the other person who will need to take action. God is at work in *their* life, and *they* will need to keep following God. However, at other times, you might sense the need to follow up by scheduling another appointment or to take more significant action if people are in danger or lacking critical needs (e.g., food, shelter, clothing) or are in the midst of crisis. If the other person does not have appropriate strength to provide what is necessary for themselves, the pastor is present to work on their behalf in the short term.

Finally, you might also decide that the right choice of action is to refer and find appropriate support. This might include contacting public authorities or other personal authorities (i.e., parents, adult children, small group leaders) in the person's life.

Conclusion

Christ hears the cries of the victims, dying *with* them on the cross. Christ hears the wails of the repentant perpetrators, dying *in their place* on the cross. Christ hears the weeping of the mourning mother and grieving friend, dying *for* them on the cross. The reconciling work of Jesus, our Great Shepherd, makes it possible for us to listen and helps our listening to be redemptive. Because Christ dies with the victim, in the perpetrator's place, and for his friends, we are enabled to listen to the world Jesus so loves in the particular person he has brought near in the moment.

Chapter 3
Clarify

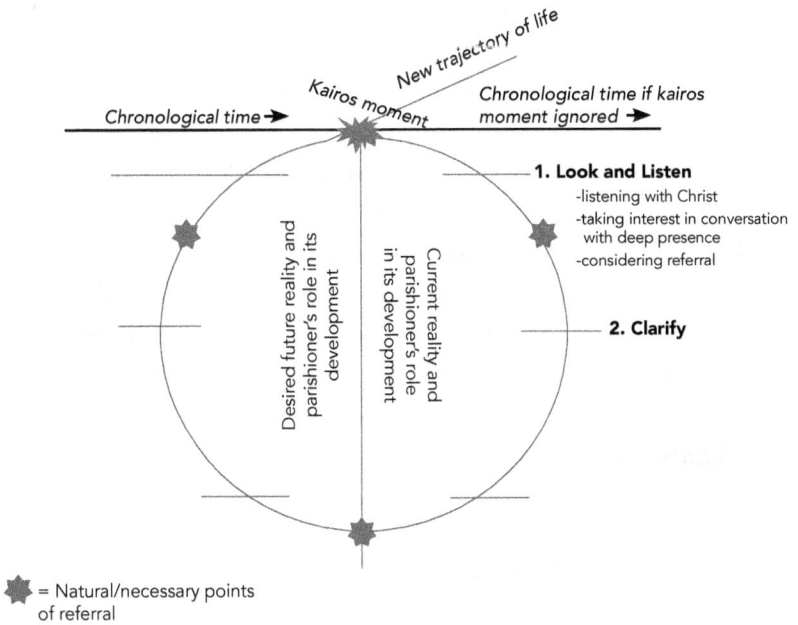

Dust/Jackets

"I like your jacket," the complete stranger said. Well, I guess he wasn't a complete stranger. I knew his name from the conference tag pinned to his

Chapter 3

tweed coat. I was attending a particular conference for the first time, feeling a bit anxious and out of my professional league. I didn't even know what league this was; I just felt like I hadn't yet made it. I was feeling like a stranger.

"Hmm? Oh, thanks. It belonged to my dad. He passed away almost a year ago. I wear it to remember him," I responded.

"Wow. I just always thought those were cool jackets. That's a much better reason to like it."

My fast friend had used his own comfort at a conference he had previously attended to help set me at ease. When the first dialogue assignment started, my jacket-fan-turned-friend caught my eye, and we engaged each other with the guided exercise from the presenter. He was a true listener, deeply engaged in what I was sharing with him. After he listened to my story, I listened to his. And, like me, I think he needed—or at least enjoyed—a listener.

The next day, we ended up at another breakout session together. And our conversation picked up where it left off. I was tuning in to see if God was at work in the man's life, although I didn't know his spiritual convictions. He told me of being let go from a mid-level management position most unceremoniously. After excelling for the last two years, suddenly he was expendable.

A word came to mind: *dust*. I think he had mentioned it when he described the desk behind which his boss was sitting when the hammer fell. I can't remember for sure. But the word was right on. I offered it to him. Did it describe his experience? The hazy and dazed feeling of the memory, the dryness of his emotion, and the pointlessness of his termination all coalesced around the word *dust*. By listening to his story, I was in the office with him; by testing out the word, I knew that I was imagining it rightly. That is the work of *clarifying*.

Matching Imaginations

Clarifying is about imagination touching imagination so that the experience of one is clearly and *faithfully* seen by the other. As I listen, am I hearing rightly? Am I hearing enough of what is being said? Am I understanding what is being shared? Like listening, clarifying is not always as easy as we might think!

As the miles passed by, the compact discs played on. *The Chronicles of Narnia* were strategic stories used to pass the time between snacks and naps as our family of five journeyed between my parents' home in Québec, Canada, and my family's new home in Marion, Indiana. Just before I moved from Ontario to Indiana, my dad was diagnosed with terminal cancer. Because we traveled to see him as often as we could, the stories not only provided pastime but also soothed our anxieties. Child and adult alike engaged any given story's plot, characters, setting, and scenes.

But we saw and sensed the stories differently. While our imaginations were all engaged, they didn't always match. The nature of a character, the setting of a scene, the shape of a ship, the taste of food was sometimes significantly different. We heard the same stories at the same time, but our imaginations were not identical. As we discussed the stories, our imaginations came together and started to match.

Clarifying is the process of connecting the listener's imagination with the imagination of the person sharing one's story and experience. Listening has allowed the listener inside the experience of another, giving a unique vantage point inside the story because the listener joined with Christ in his listening. The second step, clarifying, is working to match what we see and sense within the story with what the other person sees, too, making sure our imagination connects with theirs.

Clarifying is connecting the movie playing in my mind's eye with the images and sensations coming from the speaker. Imagination is the little movie of the story or experience forming in the head of the listener. Imagination is the screenplay writer whose actors are playing out the script being written as we listen. Listening allows the story into the mind in the first place. It is opening the book or starting the audio. Clarifying is sharing the screenplay so that it may be edited in real time. The imagination of the listener matches the imagination of the speaker.

Working with Words

When two people watch the same movie or read the same book or listen to the same song and then hold it before them both in a discussion, they are taking the imaginative experience and encoding it in words. Neither can

Chapter 3

see the exact imagination of the other. Words carry images and senses, imperfectly, from one imagination to be re-presented in another imagination. Listening to another person's experience is even more difficult than discussing a movie we watch together or a book we have both read. That person's experience is their own experience. It is entrusted to me with *words*.

Working with the words?[1] I grew up in a farming community, surrounded by friends and families who worked with tools, animals, hands, and material; we didn't think of *working* with *words*. If you worked with *words*, you might be thought not to be working at all! But these same farmers often sang in church, taught Sunday school, and shared their testimonies. My Uncle Hugh, a farmer at heart and in hands if ever there was one, was one of the best storytellers and singers I've ever heard! He selected, emphasized, and practiced words to achieve certain effects. He certainly worked with words.

But working with words is not like working with other materials. If you work with words for any length of time, you know that words are uniquely unpredictable. They don't always mean the same thing to people. Words *denote* meaning and words *connote* meaning. When words *denote*, they stand in for objects, emotions, experiences, and so on. When I say, "I was angry!" I am denoting a certain emotion with the word *angry*. Or when I say, "We hauled bricks in the wagon," I am denoting a certain vehicle with the word *wagon*. At the same time, these words can *carry* emotion and feeling. So, the word *angry* denotes a certain emotion, but it also *connotes* a wider range of emotions and meanings; it might even bring certain scenes to the listener's imagination that are not in the speaker's mind. The speaker may not have the same imagination about *angry* as the listener. *Angry* might mean more than an emotion to the speaker or listener. It might also mean danger or passion or violence or threat. Likewise, *wagon* might communicate a four-wheeled vehicle. But of what size? And what feelings come along with the wagon? When I hear *wagon*, I can't help but think about my little red wagon with removable guards that was a centerpiece of many playtimes. *Wagon* brings feelings that a speaker could never anticipate. Even the simplest of words with clearest denotation might have unexpected connotation.

What a challenge! The very tools we are given to clarify can also fool us into false confidence. That's why clarifying is so important. And since seeing into another's imagination is impossible, we must work with words. Good news, though! Just as working with one's hands, materials, or tools takes practice, and skill grows with practice, so can users become more proficient with words through practice. Don't become discouraged! It can be tempting to ignore the importance of clarifying. Don't become complacent!

Dust and Bubbles

Working with words is like working with dust. God created the world with words, forming and filling the world. God also created the first human out of dust of the earth (Gen 2:7 NIV; compare "topsoil" in CEB). Order and life came from words through dust. But in the Old Testament, dust is also about death, and it disintegrates into chaos.[2] So the psalmist talks about being brought to the dust of death (Ps 22:15; 104:29), and the fragility of human life is described as dust (Ps 103:14). Marvel's *Avengers* gives a fine scene of death, chaos, and fragility when Thanos disintegrates hero and villain alike into dust with the Infinity Stones. (Thanos is a play off the Greek word *Thanatos,* which means death.) Working with words is like working with dust. Words can bring order and life, but they can also be fragile.

Working with words is also like working with bubbles. Dr. Lacy Finn Borgo suggests listening for words that "bubble up" in conversation.[3] Like bubbles, some words keep floating to the surface. Just as some bubbles hang in mid-air and others are carried away, so do words come the listener's way, in our reach for a moment. Catch a bubble and you can turn it around, appreciate its beauty. Likewise, a word might carry several themes. During one particularly difficult season, an attentive listener noted that I kept using the word *wilderness.* Inside this word were several themes. Wilderness is a place where God provides. Wilderness is a dry place. Wilderness is chaotic. Wilderness is temporary. This one word allowed for the listener to clarify each of

Chapter 3

these themes. But just as dust is fragile, so are bubbles: popping under too much pressure, bursting in a moment, floating away unnoticed.

Therapy, Theory, Theology, and Tools

So how do we use words well? How do we work with these bubbly symbols to match imaginations? Let's describe four factors that combine words and the act of clarifying: therapy, theology, theory, and tools.

Therapy

Therapy is the treatment of disease, disorder, or injury through exercise, medication, remedy, or some other process for comfort, cure, health, or physical improvement. At first, therapy seems distinct from the pastor's work because we might think of specialists like physical therapists or professional counselors. The pastor, however, ponders and attends to the question, "How is this person's whole life, including their relationship with God?" The pastor's conversation attends to the deepest awareness of a human being, the elements of the person that hold the whole self together. Therapy for specific elements of the person like the mind, the body, and the memory is better referred to other professionals, not because the pastor cares for some fragmented *part* of the person that is called the "soul" but because the ailing body, mind, and memory of a person is best cared for by another healer with special training. This is also why pastoral care ought not to stop upon referral. The pastor is a trusted resource who can help heal and sustain well-being for the whole self, the soul, alongside another professional. By being deeply present as the listener, the pastor offers presence, power, and care that helps to integrate the whole self in relationship with God. Such presence is very therapeutic! The listener is conveying value and worth to the person *without saying a word*.

This is a vital lesson for pastors to learn! There is a powerful human instinct to fix things *with* our words, to say the right thing at the right time.

How many times I have sat in (what felt like powerless) silence with another, thinking, "I just don't know what to say." Sometimes saying nothing is the right thing! The pastor's deep, silent, secure presence gives space for Christ's love and grace to bring about a changed heart and life. Your presence, by the power of the Spirit through the risen Christ, is therapeutic.

Yet our words can be therapeutic, as well. As we work with words to bridge imaginations, the speaker has the care of being heard, known, and understood. The right word that identifies another's imagination can be very meaningful and comforting.

Theory

When I first went to the eye doctor, I had no idea how bad my eyesight was. The blurry images on the board were what everyone saw, right? When the doctor started putting lenses in front of my eyes, I couldn't believe how crisp and clear the images became. I could finally tell the difference between T and F (which made a big difference for some True/False questions).

Theories are like lenses: They help bring things into focus; they help us see a bit more clearly. Theories help explain actions, choices, and behaviors. Theories also help us predict. When we observe consistent patterns of behavior and then bring these patterns into a theory, it can help us predict how similar patterns will unfold.

In the clarifying stage, we are beginning to form interpretations of the story and experience being told to us. While we are holding off forming final interpretations, interpretation is beginning. Theories are grounded in certain disciplines, or fields of study. As we engage in the clarifying step, familiarity with two or three theories of human relationships can be exceedingly helpful to know how to show care and when to refer. While the pastoral listener might not be a clinical psychologist, trained to use and deploy certain theories of the human person professionally, the pastor may develop a humble, working knowledge of appropriate theories to provide care for the parishioner. Theory helps us to be better listeners as we tune our ears to what we are listening *to* and train us for what we are listening *for*.

Two helpful theories for the clarifying stage are Family Systems Theory and Attachment Theory. Murray Bowen, through his career working with

Chapter 3

families in a variety of professional settings, observed that families are not simply collections of individuals but interlocking systems that involve multiple relationships, emotions, and behaviors. As interlocking systems, family members learn to adapt to the ways of other members in order for the system to function relatively smoothly. When a pastor is listening, Bowen's Family Systems Theory helps that pastor to listen *for* certain interactions in a person's life, including the ongoing influence of an adult parent, the needs of a child, where a person was raised in birth order, or how a person learned how to handle emotions as a child. As the pastor helps the speaker clarify their story, the listener can see if the movie playing out in the imagination fits with the story and experience being shared by the speaker.[4]

Attachment Theory, developed by British psychologist John Bowlby, argues that human beings need to make significant attachments to caregivers from the earliest part of their lives. If the attachments do not occur, there will be challenges for forming significant relationships throughout their lives, even into adulthood. The pastor is listening *for* complications in relationships and patterns of disrupted or shallow relationships over time in various contexts.

Awareness of family systems and attachments does not necessarily make the pastor a psychologist. The pastor's work is the care of the whole person in relationship with God, and the pastor's presence is therapeutic when it communicates understanding. When the pastor hears deeper psychological issues that might be revealed by these (and other) theories, then referral is necessary even as the pastor offers ongoing support in a new form. In any case, pastors might work to become more and more familiar with certain theories of the human person in order to refine their support and to share wisdom that comes from a Christian way of life.

Theology

Recall the following diagram. Here is the pastor's area of expertise and care. By keeping in mind these different contexts of God's redemptive work, pastors can listen *for* certain contexts and have a stronger idea of what they are listening *to* in order to help support during the kairos moment.

Clarify

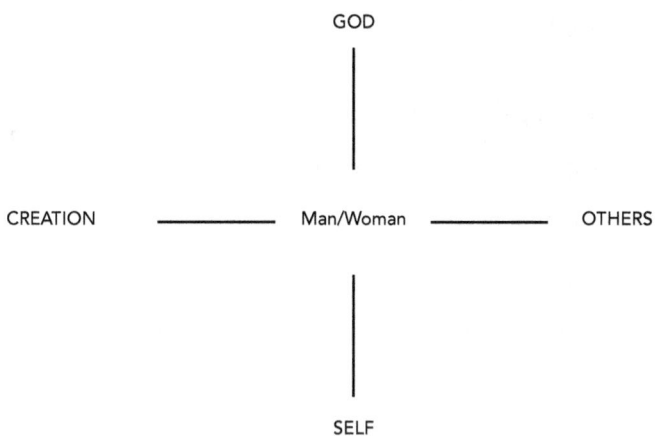

Contexts to Listen for in the Christian's Life

Each context helps a pastor by giving clues to listen *for* and cues for what is being listened *to*. Here are some examples from each context.

Creation Context:

- Meaningful work and vocation/calling
- Career change
- Further education
- Environmental implications of lifestyle
- Consumerism and purchasing habits

Others (Relationships) Context:

- Forgiveness, apology, and reconciliation
- Strained relationships
- Addictive and impulsive behavior
- Patterns in relationships
- Loneliness
- Codependent behavior
- Growing sense of responsibility

Chapter 3

Context of Self:

- Experiencing God's forgiveness[5]
- Conviction and confession of sin
- Confirmation of truth
- Coming to faith in Christ
- Support or accountability in a Christian way of life

Context of God:

- Discerning truth and justice
- Knowing God personally
- Boredom or confusion in the spiritual disciplines and the means of grace
- Unanswered prayer
- Seeking God's will and direction
- Wondering about God's presence in suffering, evil, and tragedy

Listening for cues and clues in different contexts can help the pastor to confirm a context of God's action or to consider another one. For example, a parishioner may come to speak about meaningful work and their frustration with a job, but as the conversation progresses, there is more discussion about their relationships. A change of career might provide some kind of relief or purpose, but other issues would remain: The person might have more money or a greater sense of self, but less time at home might worsen the underlying issues. The different contexts allow the pastor to attend to what issues might be hidden to the parishioner.

Just as the pastor's knowledge of personality theories helps to give cues and clues, so can theological beliefs or spiritual practices help the pastor to know what they are listening *to* and listening *for*. With this foundation in place, we can turn to some specific tools to use when working with words.

Tools

Efficiency without proficiency is risky. Speed without skill is dangerous. Tools are best used to make some work possible and to make proficient workers more efficient. A handsaw makes a construction project possible for the proficient worker. A power saw helps to accomplish the same project more quickly (efficiency). But lousy carpenters won't be any better with power tools than with hand tools. They simply have more power to do more damage.

A pastor must first be proficient before aiming at being efficient. Pastors who aim to be efficient (speedy) without being proficient (skilled) will be dangerous. Tools won't add skill to the pastoral life. The skilled pastor will use tools well and wisely. The following tools help the pastor be *efficient* in the clarifying stage and help bring it about in a time-sensitive nature. The pastor is not offering ongoing, indefinite counsel, so clarifying must happen in a time-sensitive way. Keep in mind that clarifying is about matching imaginations. You can't listen in a hurry, but the proficient listening pastor can speed up the clarifying process. Here are three tools to work with words:

Confirming Questions

Once you have a sense of what you are listening to, and you have a sense of the movie (fragmented or coherent) playing out in your imagination, you might ask for confirmation. Some questions might be phrased, "Do you mean . . . ?" "Are you saying . . . ?" or "I see [e.g., the theme of worry]. Do you see the same theme?"

Keep in mind this is not about correcting the speaker's understanding or judging their interpretation. What you hear and see is not what they must agree to. It is possible that you see something that the speaker has not yet realized—and may only come to realize upon further reflection, once this meeting is over. Confirming questions are aimed at bridging imaginations so that what you are hearing is what is being shared.

Chapter 3

Paraphrasing

Paraphrasing is taking the content from the speaker and rephrasing it in your own words. If the speaker agrees, then there is clarity; if the speaker tweaks something, then there is also clarity. If the speaker completely disagrees, then you know you weren't clear to begin with! When paraphrasing, it is important to identify the emotion of the speaker. Use new words, but match the heart of the message. Paraphrasing is particularly helpful when there have been complex scenarios or profound emotions. Paraphrasing is not stopping the movie to analyze it, but a brief pause to make sure that imaginations are staying in sync.

Summarizing

Summarizing means taking a relatively large amount of material and condensing it. A listener might be engaged in active listening for fifteen to twenty minutes and then summarize what has been shared in a couple of minutes. Summarizing is longer than paraphrasing. Summarizing is not about capturing or confirming all the details that have been shared but about drawing things together so that themes or patterns can be more easily observed. It can help to keep notes on some details for future reference and reflection.

Questioning, paraphrasing, and summarizing avoid making judgments or offering profound insights. These tools match or bridge imaginations. Clarifying is a kind of testing. As you listen, listen for key words. If the kairos model is being deployed over a set of structured meetings, review your notes from the first session. Perhaps a word from the first listening session comes back in a different way in the second. As you are listening, do you hear words that get repeated? Are there words that seem to pop up with a kind of importance but then fade away? In the clarification phase, test the word. Does it light up the eyes of the speaker? Do they latch onto it and run with it? Does it move their story forward or illuminate something they missed? The tools of questioning, paraphrasing, and summarizing can also be helpful ways to prime a future session or to encourage further sharing if the speaker gets stuck.

Challenges to Clarifying

As mentioned earlier, words are like dust and bubbles. Words bring order and words are fragile; words carry and are also carried. Human beings are similar! Human beings are made from the dust of the earth and have the spirit of God breathed into their bodies. Like words, human beings are fragile. Like bubbles, human beings are carried by another person's life and energy or by a wider culture and community. As a result, pastors must maintain humility in the clarifying stage.

How do we remain humble?

First, *remember that there is always more to know.* Regardless of how much the person has shared and how deeply you have listened and skillfully you have clarified, there is still much that you don't know. While scientific insight about the mental health of the human personality has never been greater or gone deeper, sentient human beings remain mysterious. We know about the complexity of human life through neurobiology, sociology, psychology, genetics, and other fields of study, yet there is always a uniqueness to *this* story being told, to *this* person seeking pastoral care.

When matching or bridging imagination, we must avoid the superior attitude of "I know this story." When Nathanael scoffed at Jesus's messianic credentials because he came from Nazareth (John 1:46), he demonstrated this error. It is prejudicial to think that because we know *one* thing about someone that we know *everything* about that person. We don't know everything about a person. But God does. In contrast to Nathanael's folly, there is Jesus's true, deep knowledge. Nathanael, on the one hand, hears Jesus is from Nazareth and writes him off. Jesus, on the other hand, has seen Nathanael beneath the fig tree (John 1:48), knowing Nathanael's deepest desires and longings, just as God saw through the fig leaves covering the first man and woman at creation. As we listen deeply and clarify skillfully, we humbly remember that we don't know everything but that present with us is One who does.

Second, *remember that our imaginations are already formed and are always forming interpretations.* Just as I form the images of characters in my mind as I listen, I am assigning them layers of meaning, places within the story. As the listener, you have been drawn into the story and are now clarifying from within it. But at the same time, inside *you* is an imagination. You are always clarifying from your own vantage point and with your own lenses. It's impossible to listen with absolute objectivity.

While we must be aware of this subjectivity, we also have faith that our imaginations can be *formed*—and formed properly. The Spirit of God is able to shape and form our imaginations, so we remain mindful that we are dependent upon the Spirit for wisdom in our listening and clarifying work. The spiritual formation of the pastor will have deep benefits in the kairos process.

Conclusion

During high school, a brave physics teacher tried to teach us the observer effect. The idea was that I could know the speed of something or I could know the position of something. If I figured out the speed, I altered the position; if I figured out the position, I altered the speed. Just by observing it, I was changing whatever I was looking at. When we are listening and clarifying, we are already altering the story. We are witnesses to the work God is doing. It might not yet be clear what God is up to, but the pastor who is listening and clarifying is making clear to the speaker that God is already inside the story! That God is already at work! As we listen and clarify, we know more about the story and God is altering the story.

God changes the story simply because the pastor is present, attentively listening. My daughter evoked this principle when she said, "Daddy, it's better to be afraid with somebody than to be afraid alone." Simply being *there*, in the fear, changes the fear. It's already better when someone else is there even if nothing else has changed about the situation. In one way, the experience of fear is the same; but in another way, it's now completely different. Clarifying is looking at the story from the inside and making sure that what I think I'm seeing fits with what the person living the story is experiencing. The story *is not the same* as it was without the listener, and clarifying keeps changing the story! The next step in chapter 4 adds your own voice and story.

Chapter 4

Conference

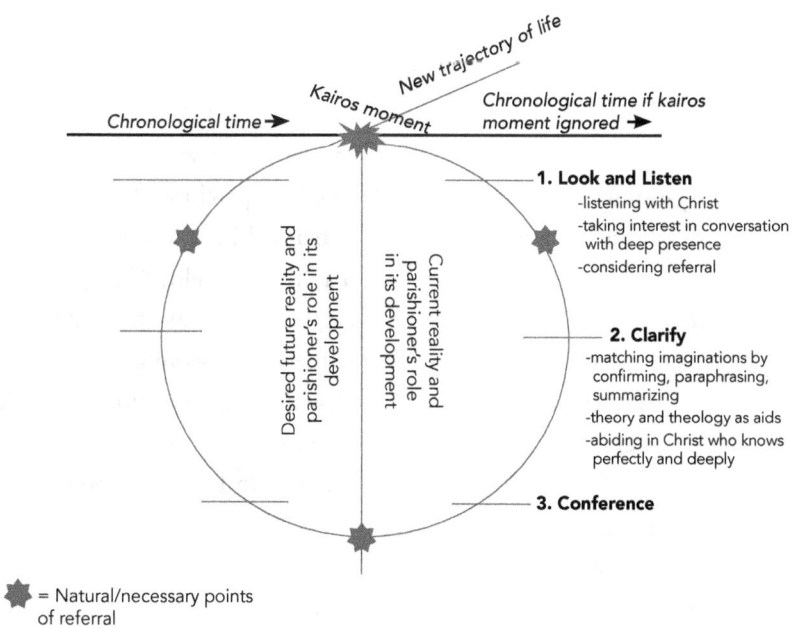

The Tipping Point

Have you ever sat next to a previously eager friend or suddenly timid child as your roller coaster cart neared the track's initial crest? The scenery

Chapter 4

is pleasant as you go up, but it's about to get terrifying as you race down. Every herky-jerky click of the cart's chains hauls the coaster closer and closer, inch by inch, to the precipice. At some point, it's clear: this coaster is getting higher and higher and it's not coming back down in the same controlled manner. The courage that seemed ample before—perhaps ramped up because you were with them—has been left somewhere along the incline. If you've ever sat next to this person, then you might know what it's like to get blamed at this point in the ride. Your seatmate is a few hundred feet in the air, strapped in by a wiggly bar (and did the operator *really* secure it?), with nowhere to go but down. And before that person gets back to safety, it's going to be a terror.

And, somehow, it's all your fault!

Like the roller coaster having just tipped over the edge, things are gaining momentum at this point of the kairos moment. Clarity and conviction have allowed, to this point, a really good vent session or a couple of therapeutic conversations, but now the person can feel, "Oh my! Now I might really need to do something." While the coaster looked really fun from the ground, now it's clear what so much of that climbing work was for. And just like the coaster-riding companion can be blamed for perching the person in this precarious position, so the pastor can be blamed here too. But why? What occurred for the pastor to be perceived in a different light? *Change is difficult, and equilibrium is (at least somewhat) comfortable.*[1] Now the pastor has listened to what needs changing and has clarified the discomfort.

When my back is out of alignment—which happens more often than I would like—I am desperate to get into a comfortable position. And when I'm in that comfortable position, *I don't move.* Nor do I want anybody to move me! Nudge me and I will bare my teeth. Touch even so much as the cushion six inches from my foot, and I will send you a cease-and-desist stare. Any jostling endangers the vital comfort. Similarly, the person in the kairos moment is in the midst of some kind of pain; that's why they have sought you out. Something is out of alignment. While the pastor has provided temporary therapy—listening and clarifying has honored the person and communicated deep value—the parishioner is sensing that they were not meant to stay in this position. But if they dare to move, the pain might return. And who's there to help them move? You. (If you are in a position of organizational leadership, then there might also be ripple effects through the church, which can also cause strain and stress in the midst of the kairos moment. We will address this further in chapter 6.)

Expect a growing sense of responsibility for the person in the kairos moment. It will take effort and courage to shift their life's trajectory. It will be tempting to keep things "normal"—to maintain a state of equilibrium. But "normal" is no longer sustainable, desirable, or acceptable! "Normal" needs to change, and to change it there will be disequilibrium. If things are going to change, things (and actions) are going change!

But the coaster hasn't yet tipped. The climb to the top still isn't complete. Unlike the roller coaster, people can still quit the kairos ride. And they might need to. Perhaps it is not yet the right time, but this was a kind of warm-up, an introduction to a necessary process. Don't feel the obligation to force it. But if they're ready, and the timing is right, then you have a defined role in helping them get to the tipping point. Conferencing happens when the pastor gets into the coaster at this point, so that the person is not alone in this work. They won't get there alone, and they shouldn't go it alone, either.

Conferencing

Conferencing is the final step for interpreting what God is doing in a person's life. The observational work of step 1 (Look and Listen) and step 2 (Clarify) is now coalescing for step 3 (Conference). Sensing that God's presence is active, the parishioner has sought out the pastor. The pastor's own story, experience, knowledge, and voice are now potentially helpful.

Christians have been conferencing from the very earliest stages. In the book of Acts when the early church was deciding whether followers of Jesus needed to become Jews in order to belong to the Way, they came together in council (Acts 15). When believers and followers of Jesus need wisdom, they connect with other believers.

Methodist historian Kevin Watson says, "Christian Conference was honest, direct, piercing conversation with other Christians that was intended to help the participants grow in holiness."[2] While Watson is addressing the practice of gathering corporately either to examine the fruitfulness of the church as a body or to describe when Methodists gather in small accountability groups, three words in the statement apply to this one-on-one context: *Christian, conversation,* and *holiness.*

- Christian: Don't shy away from the shared Christian life in this moment. Conferencing is done responsibly and effectively by the pastor who is aware of the work, word, and will of God. A sound interpretation of God's guidance for the other person is informed by recognizing God's work in the person and by careful understanding of how scripture affects the person's story.

- Conversation: Conferencing is a two-way street. Whereas earlier in the kairos moment, there was mostly one-way verbal communication, now there will be two-way verbal communication.

- Holiness: God's desire for every person is to be like Christ, to express faithfulness like Jesus, to have complete love for every person, and to serve God in God's mission of transforming the world. Not only is it God's expectation for *them,* but it is God's will for *you.* Conferencing is an opportunity for both parties to become like Jesus.

Conference Crashing

Now that we have a sense of conferencing, let's focus on some hindrances to conferencing. I have already mentioned the parishioner's natural desire for equilibrium. Shrinking away from changing the "normal" can keep the kairos moment from the tipping point. A desire for equilibrium, protecting the status quo, can take several forms.

Delayed or cancelled meetings. If the kairos moment evolved in a formal or semi-formal setting with a planned set of appointments, then take notice if the third session is delayed or canceled. The person might not be ready to go over the roller coaster's peak, but neither are they ready to get off the coaster. Now, if this happens once, you might not comment except to make sure that a follow-up appointment gets scheduled. If it gets delayed or cancelled a second time, then tactfully and gently ask if there is something keeping the person from continuing. Stay in the listening and clarifying stages during this communication. Finally, make sure that the person knows it is their responsibility to schedule another appointment.

Once reconnected, test whether there is movement in the kairos process or whether the other expects listening and clarifying work to continue. If the first two steps are expected to be repeated without a sense of moving toward some kind of change, then it might be a time to move away from counsel or to discern whether referral is needed. Counsel is about facilitating change, and if progress is not happening, then a new arrangement should be formed. The new arrangement is not about kicking the person to the curb, but the pastoral counselor can't work harder than the person whom they are counseling, nor can they facilitate the person staying in the current state.

"Go away." It is rarely said so abruptly, but the anxiety a person experiences when "normal" is threatened can take the form of an overt rejection of the pastor. You've come to the top of the coaster, they're getting off, and you're never taking them there again. Here it can be tempting to think the pastor has done something wrong, alienating the person because of unprofessionalism or another kind of failure.

Avoid two errors here. The first error is to *chase* the parishioner, initiating a reconciliation (even multiple times) that is not the pastor's role to initiate. Sometimes the other person has developed a passive-aggressive habit of inducing conflict so that others feel obligated to initiate reconciliation. In this case, the very change needed in the person's life is contritely ceasing or repenting of such manipulative behavior. It is harmful to themselves and to others. The second error is to *condemn* the person, to look for fault and failure in their conduct and attitude. Condemning the person will make it more difficult to receive them with forgiveness should they change their behavior and offer apology.

When faced with frustrating situations, I speak with a person who acts like what Wayne Cordeiro calls a "lightning rod." Just as a lightning rod takes all the energy of the lightning bolt and grounds it, this person simply *listens to*

Chapter 4

me. The actual lightning rod in my life is a pastor and friend who lives several hundred miles away, who listens to my frustration but takes no action. Lightning rods shouldn't have any connection with the situation or else there can be a nasty triangulation effect. They should be from another church, another denomination, another state—whatever significantly distances them from the situation. Ideally, the lightning rod will have the permission and skills to clarify and conference with you to see if you have done something that can be corrected or have suffered offense that needs to be addressed.

Slip away. The more polite version of "Go away" is withdrawal. The person who initially sought you out might now quit serving in ministries and leadership positions or withdraw from church attendance. While it might seem subtle, people can also change their seating positions in church, moving further away from the pastor. Keeping good records of your formal and informal pastoral conversations is vital to follow up in such situations. It can be helpful to elicit the support of others (without disclosing confidential information) in reaching out to those who have slipped away, asking the support person to follow up. For example, after engaging in listening and clarifying set a reminder for you or another mature Christian or staff pastor to check-in with the parishioner at one, three, and/or six months. This isn't an appointment, but personal accountability to have some kind of pastoral communication.

Of course, pastors can make professional mistakes. Pastors can mishandle situations, even with the best of intentions. If a person with whom you were in pastoral relationship or pastoral counsel tells you to "go away" or slips away, it is possible that such a mistake was made. Time spent praying, studying scripture, or receiving Holy Communion might alert you to such a shortcoming and you might be led to make amends. You might not be solely at fault, but you still have some responsibility to bear. A kairos moment of your own might even be happening! If you get such a nudge, pay critical attention: Ask questions of it and, strange as it sounds, *doubt* it. If it persists, seek out a trusted, wise colleague who is appropriately disconnected from the situation to gain their perspective. If they believe it could be of the Lord and the conviction still persists, then take intentional steps to be responsible and to own your error.

Sabotage. Especially if you are in a position of organizational leadership as the lead pastor or leader of a ministry department or team, a parishioner's anxiety about a change in "normal" can take the form of sabotage. The person that the pastor has been listening to and with whom they have been clarifying might become actively or passively engaged in discrediting the pastor. By discrediting the pastor, the (perceived) threat to "normal" can be averted. The pastor is no longer a person to be trusted, so the hard work of change can be avoided. Sabotage can also relieve interpersonal anxiety by initiating or strengthening relationships among those already against the pastor. The person can engage in passive sabotage by aligning and allying with others who already view the pastor with suspicion.

Pastor John Cena?

The pastor can also be hindered from conferencing. Think of it like this. Before leaning into the ropes and cocking his fist to deliver a "five-knuckle-shuffle," John Cena waves his hand in front of the closed eyes of his defeated opponent who lies helpless on the mat.[3] Right on cue, the eager crowd shouts out, "You can't see me!" Don't be too alarmed. It's "professional" wrestling, and it's actually fake in a real way or real in a fake way; I'm not sure. But if things have progressed this far in the kairos moment, they're actually getting real. The pastor has listened and clarified. It's time to make tentative interpretations of what is going on and to start moving toward taking careful, clear, and strategic corrective action. And at just this conferencing point, it's most tempting for the pastor to become John Cena and to say, "You can't see me."

Up to now in the kairos process, the pastor has kept the focus on the parishioner. The pastor hasn't been hiding but also hasn't been seen. But since conferencing involves the pastor's own story, experience, knowledge, and wisdom, the pastor's voice is part of the conferencing step. The pastor needs to be *seen and heard*. But it's not easy to join with the parishioner. While the pastor is not waving her hand in front of the parishioner, saying

Chapter 4

"You can't see me" like John Cena, yet from across the desk, chair, or table the pastor can hide.

The temptation to hide does not emerge because pastors want to *deliver* the five-knuckle-shuffle, but because, too often, they've been *hit* by one. Pastors have been on the receiving end of a blindside sucker punches (active sabotage); their stories have been used as gossip (passive sabotage); they've felt the stinging points of relational triangles. Pastors have been rejected (go away) and can feel forgotten (slip away). It's a real and legitimate concern, and it's a natural instinct to hide. Hiding protects us.

The previous section went into detail about when the other person might resist conferencing. But the pastor can also resist conferencing. Any disclosure is a risk, so conferencing must be done wisely and critically. It's natural to engage cautiously. It can take time to assess whether a person can be trusted with the pastor's story and experiences. This is happening through the listening and clarifying stages. Every act of entrusting oneself brings responsibility for the other. When I share something with another, my reputation is in their hands. And, frankly, not everyone is strong enough to bear the weight of another person's story, especially the story of a person in spiritual authority.

But it's not easy to tell whether a person is appropriately trustworthy. And pastors are not *always* good judges of character. Pastors have seen God transform sinners into saints, so pastors are often naturally optimistic when it comes to others and their intentions. Pastors might even hope that a person is going to be an ally in ministry, sharing the load of leadership with them. Before conferencing, then, you will need to determine whether and to what extent a person is trustworthy.

Several years ago, I went through active-shooter defense training as part of my employee orientation program. I hope I never need to use the training I received that day, but it has prompted an analogy to pastoral contexts. There are three basic actions in the event of an active shooter: run, hide, and fight. First, run fast, run far. Second, if running is not an option, hide. Third, if running *and* hiding are out of the question, then it's time to fight. The trainer said that not everyone is capable of fighting the same way. Some people find it relatively easy to strike another person. "But if you can't," he said, "grab onto the attacker's arm or hang onto their leg."

The simple set of instructions about deadly conflict is helpful as you consider conflict in conferencing. The training for flight-or-fight situations might apply to situations encountered in pastoral ministry. Sometimes a pastor needs to flee a person. Run fast and run far. Do not associate with them in personal or sensitive situations. There are other people from whom we can't run, and so we must appropriately defend ourselves, even as we seek to do no harm.[4] And sometimes we need to hide. In the conferencing moment, we are not necessarily hiding from a dangerous person; we are hiding as we reserve judgment. We don't yet know whether the other is wise or foolish, and so we are protecting ourselves.

Unhealthy and Healthy Hiding

Unhealthy hiding takes place when the *pastor distorts their own story and experience*. Distortion takes place through exaggerating or minimizing, perhaps emphasizing one's own heroic efforts or, alternatively, ignoring one's own failures. The story and experience are shared with the parishioner, but they are edited in a way that presents a misleading picture of the pastor.

Distortion might reveal the expectation that the pastor's story and experience should become normative. Pastors must not expect their story and experience to become the perfect model for their parishioners. This does not mean that pastors completely avoid modeling or offering examples but that the work of *Jesus* in pastors' lives, including through the means of grace and practiced through spiritual disciplines, is the focus. Indeed, conferencing is one of the means of grace for experiencing the presence of Jesus in the other's life.

Let's pause to consider two unhealthy relational dynamics that can intertwine with hiding: transference and countertransference. Transference happens when the parishioner places improper and unfair expectations on the pastor. For example, the pastor's attention or approval moves beyond being appreciated and valued to being essential to the parishioner. The pastor might be seen as a kind of figure who replaces another important relationship in the parishioner's life. Younger pastors might be seen and treated as the adult children of parishioners. Older pastors might be seen as mother or father figures. Pastors can withhold their own story and information as a way to protect against transference. There are reasons to maintain this boundary, which are covered below under the topic of healthy hiding.

Countertransference happens when the pastor is seeking unhealthy meaning and purpose for their own life from the parishioner seeking counsel. The pastor may be tempted to exaggerate their stories or experiences or to minimize their shortcomings and weaknesses. Will Willimon writes, "I find it important to admit that not all of my pastoral care is offered because I love God and my people. I also love myself, and my love of my people is at times a means of using my people to love myself even more!"[5] Pay attention to emerging feelings of excitement or anxiety, or to seeking undo affirmation in the counseling process as signs of countertransference.

Now, it's not always clear when transference and countertransference are occurring. It's not typically obvious when the pastor's opinion and insight matter more than they should. It's not always obvious when the natural desire to take pride in one's work and calling turns to unhealthy ego stoking. If the pastor senses that a relationship might be heading in either of these directions, then it is wise to add some oversight and accountability. Accountability in this context takes four things: appropriate mutual discipline (between pastor and the pastor's overseer) to communicate regularly, the permission of the pastor and the ability of the overseer to ask difficult questions, the overseer's discernment to sense incomplete truths, and clear action steps in the event of risky or wrong behavior.

Unhealthy hiding also happens when the pastor *attends to some parishioners but not to others.* This might take the form of attending only to kairos moments of parishioners that are manifest in certain contexts. The pastor might not often attend to people with workplace struggles or the pastor might not often attend to people with relationship opportunities.

Recall the following diagram.

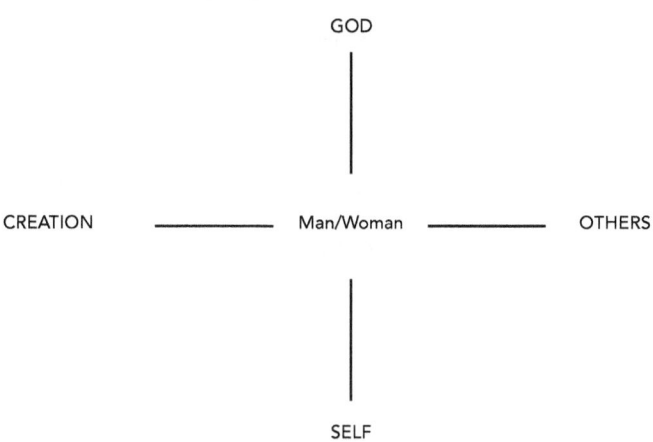

Contexts of Previous Counseling to Consider

Try to recall the last five or six times you have offered pastoral counsel. This might be formal or informal counsel. Draw the diagram for yourself and sketch the names of the counseled in the appropriate location. Does a pattern emerge? Keep this as a working compass. If, over the next twelve to eighteen months, you find yourself only dealing with the same kairos contexts, seek a trusted friend to work out whether the pattern is accidental or whether you might be engaged in hiding from a certain segment of those in your pastoral charge.

Healthy hiding, however, involves withholding elements of one's own story, experience, opinion, and relationships until the other person is believed to be wise and trustworthy. Here are some helpful tools to continue listening and clarifying, even as you reserve conferencing.[6] If a person asks you directly about elements of your life, relationships, or experiences, you might try these techniques:

Reflect:
Q: "Have you ever been abused?"
R: "It sounds like safe relationships are important to you."

Q: "Do you believe that God sends people to hell?"

R: "You take justice/mercy/fairness seriously."

Deflect:
Q: "Have you ever lost a parent?"

R: "Tell me about your relationship with your parents."

Q: "Do you think I'll see my dead friend again?"

R: "I'd like to hear about your friend."

Confirm without disclosure:
Q: "Do you ever get into big fights with your wife?"

R: "I certainly have things to work on as a husband."

Q: "Have you ever been fired?"

R: "I have not always been a model employee."

Form allegiance:
Q: "Do any of your friends experience same-sex attraction?"

R: "I am interested in helping all people come to know and follow Jesus."

Q: "Have you ever experienced racism?"

R: "I want to listen to all people who have been treated unfairly."[7]

When I keep from conferencing or only conference tentatively, I am withholding elements of my story, experience, and wisdom until I believe that what I share will be properly handled and will be appropriate to the parishioner. Here are some questions to consider as you determine the wisdom of conferencing:

- Should I trust this person to protect my reputation? Do I trust the person?

   Entrusting my story, experience, and wisdom to another person is a vulnerable moment requiring mutual confidence. If I don't trust the person, then I shouldn't share my experience with them.

- Does this person want to make a good interpretation of the kairos moment?

The person who wishes to make a good interpretation and follow the unfolding work of God is a humble person. Conference with humble people. Be careful with arrogant people.

- Is this person willing to accept my pastoral guidance and spiritual direction?

  Receiving guidance requires mutual respect. If your wisdom is sought, but you become convinced that it won't be seriously considered, then you are possibly being flattered or manipulated. Benefiting from pastoral counsel requires openness to the pastor's guidance.

Answers to these questions are not always clear, but test your confidence before engaging in conferencing. If you are confident that you are conversing with a teachable person, then you can proceed to the act of conferencing.

Wise Conferencing

What does wise Christian conferencing look like? Conferencing in the kairos model is communicating God's word in a two-way conversation so that God's will may be discerned in another's life. With the phrase God's word, I have three things in mind. First, I often have a Bible next to me or on my phone. I read it because it is God's word. Second, I also know Jesus through practices such as reading scripture, prayer, giving thanks, worship, and Holy Communion. I listen to Jesus because he is the Eternal Word of God enfleshed. Finally, in my life are a few men and women I trust because they speak God's word to me, even—perhaps especially—when it is a challenging word. Which of these sources is God's word? They all are! God's written word, God's incarnate Word, and God's proclaimed word are all God's word. And the pastor needs each of them in the conferencing moment. Let's consider them a bit deeper.

Written Word: The Biblical Text

First, conferencing often involves God's written word, the Bible. In *Walk the Line*, the cinematic biography of Johnny Cash, Johnny's older brother,

Jack, tells Johnny why he needs to read the Bible so much. "If I'm gonna be a preacher one day, I gotta know the Bible from front to back. I mean, you can't help nobody if you can't tell 'em the right story." Wise words! The pastor engages in conferencing by teaching, telling, and reminding the parishioner of the overarching story of God's written word. This teaching includes specific genres that are not narrative (e.g., a letter or a proverb). People need to hear the written word of God—even when it is difficult.

He sat across from me, and his life was blowing up. He was vice president of a well-established company; his three children were star students. But a habit and its destructive wake, which had ended years before, was just coming to light and threatened everything. I listened, clarified, and when we started to conference, one teaching came to mind: the Apostle Paul's notion of death to self. The man's eyes brightened at the teaching of being crucified with Christ. He came into my office knowing he was dying. He left knowing that it could be the death of the old self and resurrection in Christ.

The pastor also engages in conferencing by using specific stories from God's word. The Bible is the big story of God's saving work, and many little stories within the big story reveal the kinds of persons God is saving. When pastors concentrate on the New Testament, they miss over two-thirds of the story, including many subplots that can illuminate our own experiences and the experiences of those seeking our counsel.

So, pastor, stay in the written word—the whole written word! Read it diligently, slowly, quickly, devotionally, critically, and studiously. Read it in community with others who see wisdom and correction that we miss alone. Listen to it being preached by skillful expositors. Read commentaries that not only illumine the text but do so in faith that it is God's word. Trust the Psalms, which are organized as the "little Bible" within the whole canon. The poetic verse will provide counsel and emotion we otherwise couldn't anticipate in the narratives that inspire the Psalms.

Proclaimed Word: Personal Testimony

Second, conferencing involves the pastor's own testimony: What has God done for *you*? Just as Scripture is the big salvation story containing smaller stories, in a similar way your story is a big story of God's activity with smaller stories within. Without comparing pain, what similar stories or experiences in your life might illumine, advise, encourage, or refine the other's experiences and story? How might your big story further the clarifying work already started in the parishioner's life?

Think of your whole story or its smaller stories as lenses that can be laid before the parishioner's eyes. What you share is not to displace the other's story and experiences, but to help them to understand their own story better. As a result, it might take a testimony or two or ten to connect and clarify. It's like when I visit my ophthalmologist: He asks if a lens makes images *brighter* or *sharper*. Sometimes our stories can *brighten* another's story by uplifting, encouraging, building faith, and so on, but the *meaning* of the story or experience is not clear. *That* God is at work is obvious, and my story supports that conviction, but *what* God is doing remains a mystery. At other times, a story might *sharpen* the interpretation of what is going on, but the person is still left needing some courage, patience, faith, or hope.

Recall the following diagram:

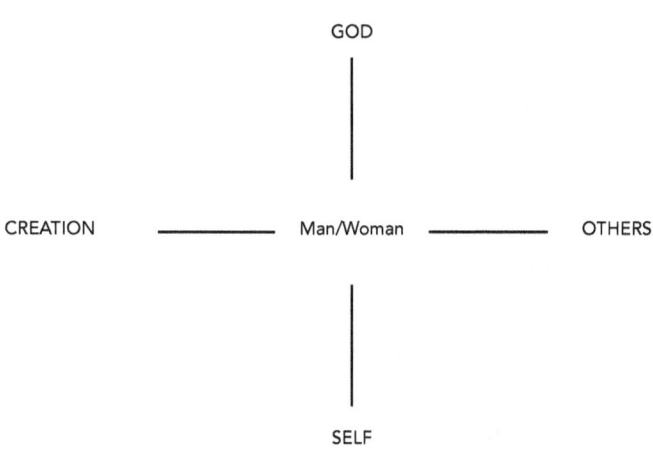

Possible Contexts of Testimony

Each of these contexts is a place to develop testimonies. Just as you practice working with the Bible's different genres, practice different testimonies from different contexts in your life. Talk about God's work in your life through your work in the world, your vocation, your environmental convictions and actions. Testify to reconciliation, forgiveness, friendship, accountability through others and the church. Speak to God's work of physical and spiritual healing in your own life, removing shame, warming your own heart strangely, giving you grace to forgive another. Finally, stay close to Jesus to share what he is sharing with you through life's journeys recently. This brings us to the incarnate Word of God.

Incarnate Word: Jesus the Teacher

The written word is only rightly interpreted in light of the incarnate Word, and testifying is always about the ongoing work of the incarnate Word by God's Holy Spirit. God's incarnate Word, Jesus Christ, is the mediator on whom we depend to provide wise pastoral counsel. He is the Great Shepherd. The risen Christ is God's wisdom at work in the world. We listen *with* Christ and *by* his work. When Christ is present, conferencing is not just a good idea or a set of best practices; it is a holy activity. It isn't holy because of what we're saying. It's holy because Jesus Christ is present by his Spirit to change hearts and relationships. Jesus makes it holy.

Just as God created by divine word in the beginning, the incarnate Word is creating a new world in the conferencing time. Will Willimon accurately describes the work of conferencing when he says, "It is an awakening to a new location, a place constructed by words that emanate from the Word."[8] As the written word and proclaimed word of God are shared, Jesus is speaking a new world into being.

I recently sat at lunch with a couple of friends—Jay and Landon. They didn't know each other; I was their connection. Jay is a brilliant scientific researcher; Landon is a brilliant pastor. I met Jay on an airplane while traveling to a conference. Whereas I wanted to sit in my uncomfortable seat with some comfortable reading, God had other plans. God's grace was moving in Jay's life. About three hours after meeting Jay, I introduced him to Jesus. Really, I just gave him the name of the person who had been making his presence known in Jay's life for some time. The lunch happened about two months later. Jay peppered me with deep, insightful, genuine questions. It was an energizing conversation! But, I must admit: I was so grateful to collaborate on several questions with Pastor Landon. When I was searching for an experience or a story to illustrate a more abstract answer, Landon jumped right in to speak directly from his own life and wisdom.

And the Spirit does the same for us! While it is helpful to share my own testimony when appropriate, there are many experiences that I don't have. Parishioners have shared with me, their pastor, challenges that I have never confronted personally. Parishioners have experiences that I haven't even seen on screen. But just as Landon jumped in, so can the Spirit! It is not *my* experience that always makes a difference; it is the experience and work of the Chief Pastor, Jesus. Not only do we have the experiences of Jesus in the Gospels, we also have the poets in the Psalms. Dietrich Bonhoeffer writes, "We can and we should pray the psalms of suffering, the psalms of the passion, not in order to generate in ourselves what our hearts do not know of their own experience, not to make our own laments, but because all this suffering was real and actual in Jesus Christ, because the Man Jesus Christ suffered sickness, pain, shame, and death, because in his suffering and death all flesh suffered and died."[9] Jesus experienced all that you will ever encounter in pastoral counsel, and it is his experience that redemptively connects with the parishioner during the conferencing step.

It's good news that Jesus has all the experience we need because some human experience is heavy. Suffering, evil, and pain can weigh us down unless the Spirit makes home inside us and carries it for us. C. S. Lewis described a weight so "heavy that only humility can carry it, and [under it] the backs of the proud will be broken."[10] Suffering, evil, and pain can weigh us down unless the Spirit makes home inside us and carries it for us.

Perhaps we can think of our lack of experience as God keeping us fresh for the hard work of pastoral work, especially in counseling. The first home my wife and I bought was a fixer-upper. We lived in it for over six years, and five and a half of those years included some form of significant renovation or repair. One of the first tasks we faced as homeowners was putting on a new roof. Being a young family at a very supportive church, I was grateful for the knowledge and labor that allowed us to replace the roof with volunteers. My wife fed everyone homemade pizza, except for Wolfgang.

Chapter 4

The name *Wolfgang* brings to mind a strong, rugged man. When I actually met this real-life Wolfgang, not only was there strength and humble ruggedness, but also there was compassion, wisdom, kindness, and a deep love for the neighbor. I never thought to ask Wolfgang to help. He was around seventy years of age, and roofing is not the easiest work. But, when Wolfgang heard there was a roofing job happening, he didn't wait to be asked. He just showed up! I saw his car slide into the drive and Wolfgang stepped out with jeans and gloves. He wasn't there to observe. Within two minutes, he was up the ladder and on the roof, having just hauled half a pack of shingles with him. He had missed the pizza, but like Christ in a holy conversation, he brought fresh energy to the project. The pastor's lack of experience can be similar. Because Jesus carries all experiences with him and is present to us, the pastor can access Jesus's experience but with fresh energy to conference. Fresh faith, love, patience is given to the pastor to be deployed at just this conferencing moment alongside the wisdom of our Lord.

Conferencing Contexts

Earlier I defined conferencing as sharing God's word in two-way conversation so that God's will may be discerned in another's life. Conferencing is to help the parishioner make a good interpretation. And God's word can be God's written word, testimony to God's work, and God's incarnate Word, Jesus, who is with us. The pastor's own voice, experience, knowledge, and wisdom in God's word is shared to help bring about this good interpretation. But conferencing can take place in different atmospheres. Here are two common ones.

Conference as Playing

Conference can have the atmosphere of play. It is clear that something is being created. The sharing of God's word is synergistic. There is momentum, even excitement. It is clear a new world is being created through the conversation. This does not mean the conversation isn't serious. In his book on play, Brian Edgar writes, "Friendship with Jesus is a more mature relationship than servanthood."[11] We are at play with a friend in the conferencing moment.

Conference as Praying

Conference can have the atmosphere of prayer. Prayer attunes us to the grace of God that is already present. We pray not to *earn* grace but to *access* it. Prayer is a means of grace. Prayer is not making a deposit in God's presence but making a withdrawal from an endless account. Sometimes prayer feels like work. It is work! Conferencing is hard work, a lot of effort made possible by the favor of God that is believed to be present to keep advancing the kairos moment.

Sensing conferencing as prayer is more likely to happen as the pastor develops a sacramental worldview. Within a sacramental worldview, every conversation is a prayer. God, the giver of words, is present by the Spirit of the incarnate Word. Conferencing may even involve explicitly engaging in prayer, whether praying spontaneously or praying the scriptures or pausing to study scriptures through *lectio divina*.

Conclusion

In Matthew 9, after Jesus spent time preaching and teaching in towns and synagogues, he saw the crowds. The experience broke his heart. He had compassion on the harassed and helpless, on the thrown-about and thrown-aside (Matt 9:36). In response, Jesus told the disciples to pray for workers to be sent into the fields (9:38). And guess what! Matthew immediately tells of Jesus sending the twelve into the countryside to cast out demons, to heal diseases, and to preach.

At the same time, he warns these sent ones to be shrewd and discerning. He says to stay in people's homes, yet only to stay if people are receptive (10:11-14). He warns that they will be handed over to local councils and authorities, kings and governors (10:17-18). Today, pastors can be called into the court of public opinion, with a jury populated by social-media feeds and Twitter followers. Hurting people will still hand you over. It is not easy to spot the difference between a moment of muck or opportunity, but the compassion of our Lord compels us. He is still sending us. Shepherding people is dangerous work. Follow the advice and model of our Lord: Keep an open heart with peeled ears, enter open homes, and conference wisely.

Chapter 5

Statement of Change

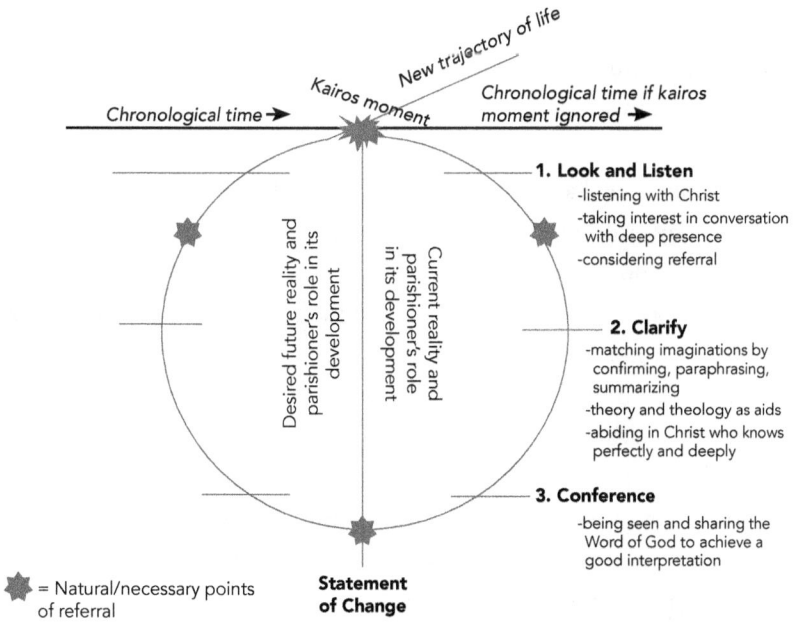

Well Digging

It wasn't the faucet. It wasn't the filter. It wasn't even the tank. After attempting my few, humble fix-it skills, I realized that no water was coming to my kitchen because the pump was broken. Not just broken. *B-r-o-k-e-n*. It needed replacing. And it wasn't an easy job. Living in the country, we had a dug well. I don't know how deep the well went into the ground, but I know how deep the well cap was because I dug it up. The dig started easy enough, but after about a foot of topsoil, I hit clay. Sticky, heavy, mucky, hard-yet-gooey clay. After chipping, scraping, and some cajoling, I finally reached the well cap. The point of digging to the cap was to add a section of pipe to extend the well above ground in order to drop in a submersible pump. It was one of those "Let's do harder work now so that we can do less work later" kind of jobs.

I am skeptical about those kinds of jobs. When I encountered a nasty plugged pipe, I asked my buddy Kevin what he would suggest: "Sell and move." When people hit the kairos moment, that's exactly when they might be tempted to move. People will rearrange significant chunks of their lives to make sure nothing changes. But if you have a person who's willing to do the work, the kairos moment might be a season of working hard now to work less later.

Through the kairos moment, you have been watching someone dig through clay. Through listening, clarifying, and conferencing, you've helped someone dig down to a well cap. Now all the digging work is going to *reveal* its purpose: naming the change that God is bringing about in this moment. I'm sure that not every well that needs digging goes through clay, but some do. Regardless of what is covering the well, it all needs to be cleared away so that there's a clear picture of the cap. What's written on the cap is the Statement of Change.

The Statement of Change can sometimes roll off the tongue quickly. All the listening and clarifying and conferencing has brought things to a crisp, clear vision of the future. At other times, another brief cycle of listening, clarifying, and conferencing might be necessary. Try paraphrasing and summarizing to see if the statement clarifies organically. You might also ask the person to work on the Statement of Change on their own time before the next session.

The Statement of Change can't be rushed and can't be overestimated. It will be the foundation for the entire second half of the kairos moment. You will need to keep coming back to it at various points of confusion, worry, and weakness. In this chapter, I will offer three components of a strong Statement of Change and a warning for what's coming when it is being pursued.

High Definition

When I was a child, we had an antenna on top of our house and a little magic box on top of the TV that turned the antenna to pick up different channels when it was in different positions. When the antenna was in the right place, it was a clear picture—well, as clear as we knew it could be. Sometimes, however, when the antenna was turning and the channel was clearing, you got two blended pictures and fuzzy sound. In contrast to my experience, my children take it for granted that their television presents every show in high definition. They don't know about the previous days of blurry TV or even standard definition. Every corner of the screen and every bit of sound is crystal clear.

High definition means that the statement is about a "particular goal."[1] For my friend in the coffee shop, it was, "I will start my own business." This goal was clear because his trade was decided. While the statement was particular, it was also fairly complex. It would take several steps to be completed. This is OK. (This is why there is a planning step to be covered in the next chapter.) The Statement of Change is the parishioner's concise, clear statement of what they intend to be in this kairos moment by the help of God. Every word and its meaning must be clear.

Humble Distance

This won't be the only kairos moment in the person's life. God will continue to work. This perspective and conviction is formed by faith and hope. We can confuse faith and hope with optimism, but they are different. Optimism might lead us to take bigger risks; faith and hope lead us to take action in light of God's will and work. Faith and hope do not determine the size of the action. Faith can be expressed in small actions, and it can be expressed in large actions. Faith and hope do not make us more optimistic; they make us humbler. In other words, the Statement of Change might be large or small, but either way it is centered on God. As the shepherd, you will need to help determine whether the Statement of Change is fitting to what God is doing *now*, while you are also believing that God will continue to do more *later*.

The Statement of Change aims to describe the change sought between current reality and the desired outcome. But before the change is accomplished, there remains a gap between reality and expectations. Here's a popular diagram of the experience.

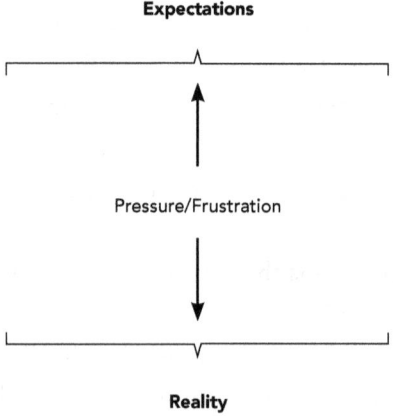

The Gap between Reality and Expectations

The gap is filled with two experiences that the person will eventually experience. First, there will be pressure. If there is no pressure, then the Statement of Change is too small or too imprecise. If the person takes their own Statement of Change sufficiently seriously, there will be pressure to achieve the new reality. Second, there will be frustration. If there is no frustration, then the Statement of Change has named a gap without sufficient challenge. All the hard work of listening, clarifying, and conferencing is validated when there are roadblocks and impediments. Frustration is the fruit of labor on this side of accomplishment.

At the same time, the distance can't be so wide that it can't be accomplished. When genuine effort and good faith are put into a faulty goal and the result is failure, cynicism takes root. Cynicism grows when expectations are not met. And cynicism is a disease. People doubt the possibility for any change when they are cynical. Cynicism damages the faithful imagination. People might lose faith that God really is *for* them; they might lose faith in their own abilities; they might lose faith in their world. And when people are cynical toward God, themselves, or the world in general, watch out. They can be dangerous with words and actions, caring little for who gets hurt. Cynicism can lead to harm.

As a result, the Statement of Change must broach a humble distance. Again, this might be a very wide distance, but it's a distance that is rooted in the will of God for *this* moment or season. Your job is to help determine and discern a humble distance.

A calendar is a wonderful tool to reflect on the humble distance. Try to put a tentative date for the Statement of Change. When might the Statement of Change be a reality? Assigning a date makes clear the range of time that includes uncertainties and variables that will possibly inhibit the statement's coming to reality.

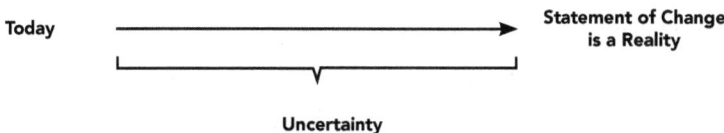

Time Range between Today and Statement of Change's Accomplishment

Your role is to help determine whether the Statement of Change reasonably fits the time line. What counts as a reasonable amount of time depends on the age and life situation of the parishioner and the nature of the statement. If you are sensing time will present a hindrance, discuss whether the distance can and should be narrowed.

Chapter 5

Now, there is one experience that should be included here. Sometimes when people have been in kairos moments before now, they are *already* frustrated. They see what God is up to and they can craft a Statement of Change, whether in writing or in their mind, but they are frustrated because they thought *it was already reality.* One common frustration is the issue of forgiveness. People would do very hard work, consciously choosing and crafting a life of forgiveness, but then come to a realize that the work of forgiveness was not yet completed—perhaps even years later. In that moment, the pastor might hear the words, "But I really thought I already forgave them! Why am I going through this again?"

The concept of a humble distance helps us to understand this experience. God *really does* bring us to points of new reality. Using the example of forgiveness, there was real and true forgiveness offered and practiced at a previous point. A new life really *has* been formed. But now God is taking the person to another level. Sometimes God preserves lives in a certain pattern until we are ready, willing, and able by God's Spirit to engage in greater, deeper transformation. The person *really had* forgiven. And now God is being gracious to allow them to engage in deeper forgiveness.[2]

Sometimes the issues that God desires to deal with in a kairos moment have been preserved in a person's life like a cyst. Rather than spreading poison through the person's self and life, the cyst has been sealed up, kept intact by God. The kairos moment is when God is allowing a little extra pressure to bring the cyst to life's surface. Care and precision in listening, clarifying, and conferencing has kept the cyst from disappearing under the surface once again. Instead, the Statement of Change starts to outline the precise lines of surgery that will lance the skin, remove the cyst, and stitch the life's skin back up. While it is frustrating that what was believed to have been dealt with earlier is making a reappearance, I also find it very pastoral to consider the situation as God's ongoing grace in God's timing. Because our parishioners can experience weak faith or low hope, how important to tend to your own soul. Your faith and hope may be enough to share with them!

Holy Destination

The pastor's role is not to support any and all change efforts the person decides to undertake. The pastor's aim is not the parishioner's self-actualization but Christlikeness. The Statement of Change must lead to a holy destination because the pastor can't support action contrary to the will of God and the Christlikeness of the person. Sondra Wheeler writes, "The fundamental question from the viewpoint of pastoral counseling is not how you as an individual can best obtain whatever you might want from your life. It is rather how you can take your place within the body of Christ and become the person God calls and empowers you to be."[3]

The pastor is not the person's hired coach or spiritual consultant. A pastor is a shepherd of the soul. At the same time, the pastor also has responsibilities, for example, to the family of the person (especially if under pastoral care in the local church), responsibilities to the local church they pastor, and to Christ. The pastor must keep each context in mind when they are supporting and considering the Statement of Change. If something seems good for an individual, but wrong for the wider family; right for a family, but wrong for a church; right for a church, but unfaithful in its witness to Christ, it is best to keep reflecting, praying, and cycling through the kairos steps.

There are times when parishioners are adamant about a change that the pastor can't support. The parishioner may invoke the conviction of their own conscience. The conscience is a powerful guide, but keep in mind that the conscience is not anyone's final authority. Consciences may be damaged and not function properly (1 Tim 4:2). God's word must remain final authority to guide the person's work of specifying God's will in the kairos moment. With this in mind, the pastor need not give up the parishioner's formation right away and be eager to refer. Disagreement might be a moment of righteous subversion to gently guide and tweak the Statement of Change.[4] A Statement of Change that the pastor does not support might be a moment of discipleship and repentance.

But the disagreement may continue. A parishioner might insist upon their will. The pastor's guidance may not be taken. Notice the star symbol in the diagram at this point in the model. The Statement of Change is a natural point of referral when the pastor can't support the parishioner's aims. If an unholy aim is formed, defended, and ultimately held, ethical referral is the pastor's next step. Ethical referral means guiding to a person whose theology and pastoral wisdom the pastor trusts. Of course, the parishioner may not accept this referral. Referral allows the pastor to maintain convictions while being humble that they may have misguided, misunderstood, or simply been wrong about the righteousness of the Statement of Change.

A Statement of Change must be high definition, cross humble distance, and pursue a holy destination. But even when these all align, I offer a final warning.

Disrupted Harmony

This final point does not directly inform the Statement of Change but it should be taken into consideration by the pastor. Remember that there is a measure of harmony that has been threatened in the conferencing step. Now that threat is becoming real. What disruptions can be anticipated that the pastor might address ahead of time? How can the pastor help to prepare the parishioner or others in their family or even in the church? Especially if the parishioner is in a position of organizational leadership, then there might also be ripple effects through the organization that may cause strain and stress in the midst of the kairos moment. This disruption may be positive too! Especially if there is a transformation in the works for a key leader in the church, there might be churchwide impact for which to watch and to plan. The pastor may even want support to handle certain organizational change. We will address this more deeply in the next chapter, but some wisdom can be applied even at this stage. If some disharmony simply looks like it will be too great to overcome, then consider revising the Statement of Change before advancing.

Conclusion

The Statement of Change can emerge quickly right after the conferencing step or throughout the conversation. It might emerge slowly through a set of meetings that have been structured according to the steps of the kairos model. Or, it might develop through a season where the kairos moment seems to have stalled. One way to start on the Statement of Change is to have the parishioner develop a statement on their own, after giving them appropriate description, and then take a session (or two) to bring it to appropriate definition, distance, and destination.

Once the Statement of Change is crafted, considered, and encouraged, a new set of skills is needed and a new kind of work begins. Some pastors are naturally gifted at the first half of the kairos moment but struggle to move into the Statement of Change and then to see new life in Christ emerge. Other pastors naturally anticipate the desired change through the entire conversation or set of pastoral counseling sessions to this point. But both sides of the model are necessary. It's no use knowing how to drop a submersible pump to draw fresh water if you're not willing to dig to the well cap. Likewise, the point of digging to the well cap is to draw fresh water. Digging and drawing are both necessary to get water. We've dug to the cap, discerned there's a clear step, and now we're going to work at drawing fresh water.

Chapter 6
Plan

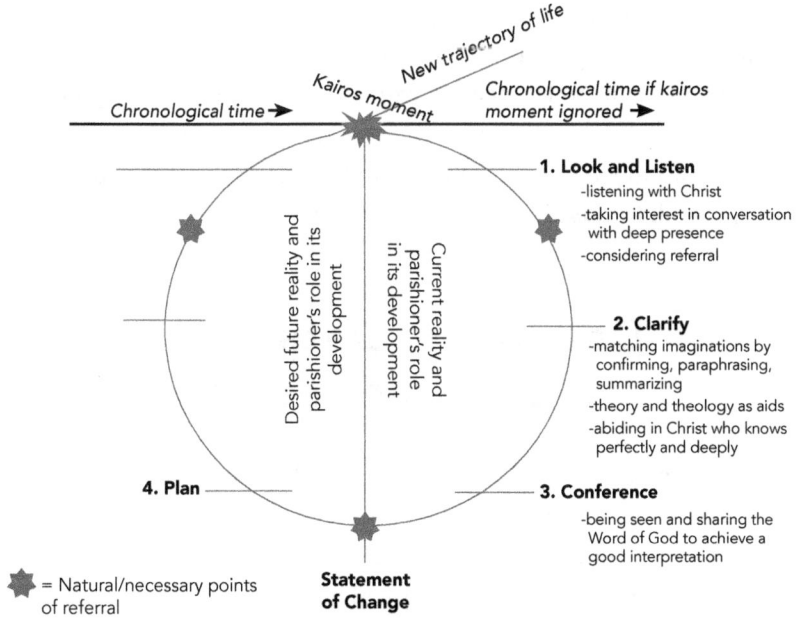

I Love It When a Plan Comes Together

The line, proudly proclaimed by the *A-Team*'s leader John "Hannibal" Smith, after some silly scheme worked to perfection just within the 48-minute

Chapter 6

TV-show time limit, was *not* what I was thinking as a whirlwind meeting was wrapping up. I was consulting for an organization, observing a department team meeting. The meeting wasn't supposed to be a whirlwind. It was supposed to be planned, ordered, and productive. As the meeting was wrapping up, however, a supervisor happened upon the meeting and jumped right in. Suddenly there was a change of course, change of strategy, change of plan. No intervention helped. I could see the thought bubble above the supervisor's head: "I love it when a plan comes together," but it was a plan he wouldn't be helping to execute. After the supervisor stepped out of the room, I saw a new thought bubble above the deflated team's collective head, "I hate it when a plan gets dumped on me."

In this chapter, I suggest a structure and present some helpful skills in developing a plan to bring about the Statement of Change. The goal is to have a plan come together through the collaborative work of the pastor and the parishioner. This can't happen if the parishioner feels like a plan has been dumped on them. So let me start with a simple reminder: Yes, you want the plan to come together. Yes, it's a beautiful thing when it comes together. But your job isn't to *produce* the plan. If you do, everything to this point might be lost. Your job is to *help the plan get produced*.

Deadlines, Details, and Differentiation

I can't be too tough on the supervisor. I've done the very same thing! I've jumped into a meeting, session, or conversation with full gusto and left someone else with an impeccable plan. Little had they known that a complete guide to their personal success had been in my head the entire time! If only they had come to me sooner! Of course, putting it like that reveals just how silly this attitude and action are. But it doesn't capture just how tempting it can be for the pastor to take over at this point in the kairos moment. The silliness doesn't offset the seduction.

Why might the pastor be tempted to jump ahead, to take charge, and to be overcontrolling at this point in the kairos conversation?

Deadlines: Prudence before Expedience

First, the pastor might take charge because she or he is dealing with *deadlines*. It is expedient to take charge. If the kairos conversation has taken a structured form across several meetings over several weeks, then at this point it can be tempting to lose momentum. You might be tempted to speed things along to make sure they are completed. But speed can be dangerous.

I helped a friend to shingle the roof of his shed. We had been working for six or seven hours. It was starting to get dark. Both of us were ready to be done and the job was almost complete. Our attention waned. But we weren't on the ground. We were still swinging hammers, hauling shingles, and pounding nails. He said, "Alright. I know we're ready to be done working, but let's be careful. We don't want to have an accident now." Wise words!

Recall one of our values from listening: just as you can't listen in a hurry, it's often unwise to plan that way, too. Instead of expedience, focus on prudence—what will *actually* bring about success. When the parishioner develops the plan, they are more likely to own it. And when they own it, it is more likely to be successful. Stay prudent in the planning phase! Developing a hasty plan can sabotage the whole process to this point. Go at a speed that the parishioner can be active in the process.

Details: Perspective through Experience

Second, the pastor might be tempted to take charge because they are familiar with planning. They have *experience*. Planning is a sweet spot for people who have organized everything from pizza parties to church services to volunteer training days to park cleanups. But now you need to make a switch. You are moving from functioning as the planner to teaching the planner. You are not doing the work; you are coaching the worker.

The combination of experience and spiritual perspective is incredibly valuable. On the one hand, you have knowledge of *details*. You can anticipate the value of schedules, routines, charts, checklists, and precision. On the other hand, you know exactly why this phrase got coined: "The devil's in the details." You've seen the devil show up. As you are working through the

Chapter 6

planning phase, use your perspective to suggest where further detail might be added and also to anticipate where the devil might be lurking.

Differentiation: Persons with (Healthy) Ego

Finally, the pastor, like every conscientious person, wants to do a good job. They have an *ego* invested. It's easy to hear *ego* in a negative sense, but by healthy ego I simply mean a healthy sense of self. A healthy ego knows its preferences, weaknesses, and challenges. A healthy ego knows where it ends and where another starts. A healthy ego knows it is different from every other person. Your skills, body, education, experience, preferences, income, and a host of other variables make you a unique individual. That's good! The parishioner has this same set of variables. They are not the same as anyone else. They are not the same as you.

It can be tempting to take control to achieve success or to feel successful, but control will doom the process at this point. We have all seen parents try to find success through their children or watched teachers self-inflate through their students. Pastors are not immune to finding meaning through the success and spiritual growth of their parishioners and churches. For the pastor in the kairos conversation: the parishioner's success or failure is not a report card on your pastoral ministry.

Recognizing and practicing these differences is the process of *differentiation*. This is a very important factor because only *one* of you will be responsible to carry out the plan. And it's not you. The pastor must work at maintaining appropriate distance from the parishioner. The pastor is working with another person, a person who is growing in their *own* responsibility. Take a look at the diagram at the start of the chapter. On this side of the kairos loop, the parishioner is defining *their* role in bringing about the new reality defined by the Statement of Change. The Statement of Change is the end goal, and the planning phase is drawing up the blueprint. Yes, the pastor might be able to develop a better plan, but if the pastor takes too strong a role in forming the plan, the parishioner's ability to take the lead role is already being undermined.

To understand difference, it's helpful to distinguish between kinds of wisdom. Some wisdom is for everyone. This wisdom can be applied in a general way across many contexts. Some wisdom is more limited. This delimited wisdom can be applied in particular situations by particular persons. Some wisdom in your life won't be wisdom for another because you're different![1] Differentiation is about humility, remembering that what fit and worked for you may not fit and work for another. But at the same time, you maintain faith that God's providence dispenses wisdom that can be found, formed, and applied. Your job, in this phase, is to help guide the plan that finds, forms, and applies wisdom correctly to the person sitting in front of you.

Fail to Plan = Plan to Fail

Have you heard the phrase "If you fail to plan, you plan to fail"? It was printed on a ruler that was coiled as a design into the agenda I was given in Grade 7. I was amazed at the design. An agenda, a ruler, and an inspiration! But I didn't use the agenda. Something kept it from being the transformative tool its designer dreamed it to be.

Even if I didn't use the slick tool for the task, the simple truth stuck with me. Good intentions without a workable plan are completely ineffective to bring about change. There needs to be a plan that is practical.

Let's put this into a formula.[2] Change happens when $D \times V \times P > R$.

D: Dissatisfaction with current reality

V: Vision of preferred future

P: Practical first steps

R: Resistance to change

Dissatisfaction, vision, and practical first steps must all be present and working together to overcome a resistance to change. Each element is necessary. D and V are powerful and necessary, but P must be present. Why? Because the formula is not about addition. Desire can be strong in the parishioner, but it is not enough to bring about lasting change. Vision is beautiful, but it is not enough to bring about lasting change. If any of the factors is

Chapter 6

missing, then the left side of the formula will be *zero*. No change. Each factor is necessary for there to be change.

First, recall that the kairos moment started with disequilibrium—a disruption that sparked desire for change (D). The conversation delved deeply in the kairos moment by looking and listening (step 1), clarifying (step 2), and conferencing (step 3). Second, see how the Statement of Change names a simple vision of the preferred future (V). We have two elements that must be present in order to overcome the resistance to change. Planning is about developing practical first steps that the parishioner can take toward achieving the Statement of Change. If there are no practical first steps, there will be no change. It is that simple. If there is a failure to plan, there is a plan to fail.

Keeping brief notes, mentioned previously in the kairos conversation, can be helpful here because passion fades and dissatisfaction wanes. Hopefully the Statement of Change is so high definition that even if it is tweaked, it remains clear. Even if the V is solid, the D can wane. People may not forget what brought them into the kairos moment, but the power of dissatisfaction can fade. Brief notes can be helpful at reminding the pastor and the parishioner of the passion and importance that was initially connected with the kairos moment.

Planning: Two Persons and Five I's

Not everyone thinks the same way. Some people think concretely and specifically. Some people think abstractly and generally. Some people think analytically, pulling things apart to think about each piece. Some people think synthetically, putting things together to think about the whole. Some people think linearly—in a straight line, one step at a time. Some people think laterally—along a slant, seeing what's coming from the side.

While not everyone thinks the same way, all thinking is valuable. In the planning step, your role is to provide counterpressure to the parishioner's natural way of thinking in order to make the plan wise and achievable. So, while any of these angles might come at various times, they all need to be included if the planning step is to be successful and effective. If the person thinks linearly, then help them to address the plan from multiple angles. If the person thinks abstractly, encourage precision and practicality. What impact will the plan have on employment? How might family react? What time of the day will be a bit more rushed?

Ideas

A plan needs to generate ideas for defined actions—things that the person will do. The parishioner needs two kinds of actions: steps and habits. Steps are one-off actions that can be completed. Habits are ongoing actions that help to orient the person as a whole. Let's take these in turn.

Steps

First, a step has three requirements:

1. A step must clearly lead to the Statement of Change. If it is not clear how the step moves toward the Statement of Change, then it might be peripheral or it might be part of a series of smaller steps leading to a larger step. If it is part of a series of steps, then make sure they align in the right direction. Part of your work is to help keep the main point the main point. Busyness can be appealing as a defense mechanism. Make sure the step clearly fits on the path to the Statement of Change.

2. A step must be able to be completed and known that it is completed.

3. A step must have a timetable.

Here are some examples of steps that fit the above: "Sharpen my resumé before our next meeting," "Learn how to use Google Docs tonight," "Get a part-time job by June 15," "Speak with my wife about our son before Thursday."

Each of these steps involves a measure of interpretation. Someone might learn Google Docs to a bare minimum, and exactly what counts as "sharpening" one's resumé will be up to the person doing the sharpening. Depending on factors like motivation, learning ability, and cultural intelligence, steps might need more specificity. For example, "speak with my wife about our son" might be a larger step that presumes setting a time to do so. Just as the Statement of Change needs clear definition, steps need to be appropriately clear. Press for specificity as needed for accountability, but remember the parishioner is the one doing the work. (If the steps aren't being completed on time, consider whether more specificity is needed. We will cover this in more depth in the next chapter.)

Don't take for granted that smaller steps are clear to the person in the kairos moment. You might sense that a well-defined shorter step or two would be beneficial. Even the most intelligent and competent person might need smaller, clearer steps to make progress. When I first served in a service club in my church's town, I had no idea how to operate within their system. Because I was the youngest member, I was given charge of the youth services committee. After a year, I had accomplished precisely *nothing*. I had no idea how to get started. It took someone walking through the processes and offering tangible ideas to get me started in the work. I was able to get the job done, but I needed smaller steps to become familiar with the committee's mandate, and the club's communication tools in order to form the right team and to call a meeting. Even the most competent people might need smaller, clearer steps to make progress in new contexts.

Habits

Second, the person ought to consider developing one or two keystone habits.[3] A keystone habit is a specific, ongoing action that helps to form a person's disposition and character so that all other actions are affected or made possible. A keystone habit might be a spiritual discipline, such as prayer, scripture reading, fasting, or confession. Ongoing corporate worship is an important keystone habit to maintain or develop alongside other steps and habits.

Let's look at the relationship between steps and habits. In the previous chapter, I encouraged assigning a tentative date to the Statement of Change in order to consider its reasonable chance of success. The point of setting a date is not about strict accountability, but about assessing the nature of the Statement of Change.

Plan

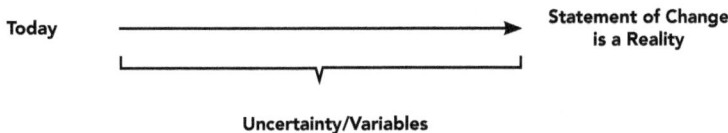

Let's modify the diagram above to capture this relationship between steps and habits.[4] Professor and business consultant Amy Webb points out that the further you project into the future, the less predictable it becomes. We have more evidence and data to predict next week than we do to predict next month or next year. As a result, Webb encourages her clients to focus on *preparation* instead of *prediction*. Because of the time-limited nature of the Statement of Change and the time-sensitive component of the steps, we are obviously doing a humble amount of predicting. Through this process of discernment and by faith in God, the parishioner has named some steps that they believe can be taken in a time frame that will lead to specific life change. But we can't ignore that the future is unpredictable. We might need to modify steps. And we might change expectations for when the Statement of Change might be completed. (We will explore this more in the next chapter.) In contrast to steps and the Statement of Change, however, habits are more secure.

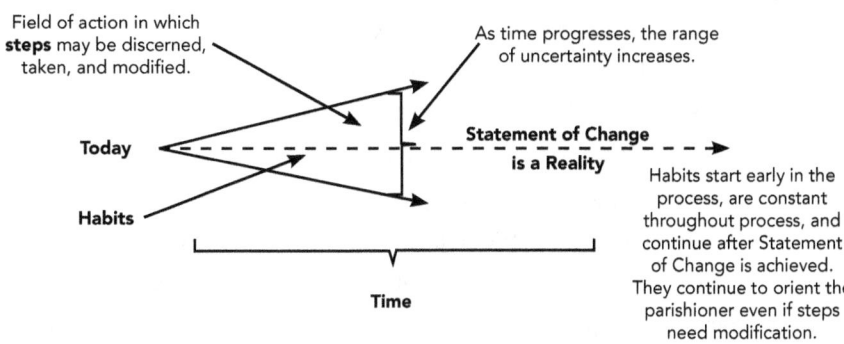

Relationship between Steps and Habits

Chapter 6

Notice how we've broadened the time *line* to be a time *triangle*. The triangle symbolizes the complexity of reality; the span of time allows a range of uncertainty, even while we remain aimed at the Statement of Change. Rarely do things go *exactly* according to plan; so rather than a straight line, then, the triangle forms a "field" of action.

During my first week on the job in my first church, John noticed I was not married and in need of friendship, so he invited me to breakfast on my first Saturday in town. He would pick me up at 8:00 a.m. I hadn't yet secured an apartment, so I was staying at the senior pastor's house. I woke about 6:30 a.m., dressed, and went to check email and read the news. It was 7:15 a.m. I know what time it was because that's when the car horn started honking. I thought, "Whoa! 8:00 a.m. already?" and checked the time. "Nope. Can't be John. Too early." The horn honked again. I figured I should go and check. Sure enough, there was John, honking to let me know he had arrived.

What followed was a standing Saturday breakfast date that lasted for two years. John listened to work, hobbies, personal projects. As a full-time large construction project advisor at a local state university, John was familiar with plans. He was also familiar with their breakdown. Any time a plan needed tweaking, John would simply say, "Field conditions!" Even when the plan accounted for contingencies, some conditions only came out in the field.

I had a plan for that first Saturday morning. A honking horn changed it. The plan got changed by a man familiar with changing plans. "Field conditions!" Likewise with any plan developed for a Statement of Change, there will be "field conditions," contingencies will emerge.

Alongside the field of action there remains a plumb line of habits. Habits start early in the process and remain constant, even beyond the Statement of Change. Ongoing spiritual growth might include adopting new spiritual disciplines or habits. While steps should be adapted to field conditions, habits help to make the person adaptable. For pastors, familiarity with the range of spiritual disciplines grounded in the history of the Christian faith can be very beneficial as they provide counsel and support. Different disciplines might provide more appropriate personal habits and clear connection with the Statement of Change. Again, encourage one or two keystone habits or disciplines. The goal is to provide stability throughout the process and *not* to overwhelm in what likely remains a delicate time of life.

Finally, keep your eyes open for things that knock habits out of plumb. Are the steps ethically faithful to a life conformed to expectations established by Christ? Do they present temptations, warnings, concerns, or risks to the life of faith? Do the habits foster a coherent and stable life in Christ? It is a tremendous privilege as a pastor to show how a person's *own* discerned action steps or habits help to orient them to God! When a person realizes that God has been directing them and giving them wisdom and insight, it can be inspiring. To the extent the parishioner has formed the steps and habits, they will have greater ownership of the process.

Inventory

One of my earliest jobs was counting inventory. My entrepreneurial aunt owned a shoe store and recruited me to help count inventory. My brother and I were to take stock of the store's goods and their value. I think she realized her mistake fairly quickly. Counting inventory requires a balance of speed and precision. I was neither fast nor precise. One of the first jobs I ever lost was counting inventory.

But the lesson proved quite helpful in my pastoral leadership. Every person I ever encountered in a kairos moment already has had resources in his or her life that are relevant to achieving the Statement of Change. Like counting for a retail store, taking inventory requires a balance of speed and precision. An entire audit of a person's life is not possible, but an audit of a few areas might prove resourceful.

A plan requires having a general knowledge of a person's inventory, including:

- Relevant practical skills. What does the person know how to do? Are they proficient with internet research? Do they play a musical instrument? Can they read quickly?
- Models to follow. WWJD? The popular bracelet from the 1990s (based on Charles Sheldon's book from 1896) aimed to raise ethical living by reminding the wearer that Jesus was a model.

Not only is there Jesus, but also there might be a parent, sibling, friend, or another model in the person's life. The model might be a fictional character or a historical person, now deceased. Be mindful whether the potential model has certain traits or abilities not shared by the parishioner. Think through how the person will serve as a model. Important but unique characteristics that have led to their success will be difficult to emulate or replicate. Exceptional people are often not ideal models, but rather outliers whose lives can't be emulated easily. Help the parishioner determine what about the selected model may be formed in their own life.

- Knowledge/education. What has the person studied, formally and informally, that might be relevant in forming a plan to achieve the Statement of Change?

- Patterns or rhythms of life. Does the person have a rhythm or routine that can be harnessed to put the plan into play? A rhythm and routine can also help to make the plan even more concrete. For example, any step that will take a reasonable amount of time requires eliminating the equivalent amount of time from the person's schedule. This might be easily seen if the person starts working a part-time job at twelve hours a week. But other actions are not as easily quantified. For example, perhaps the Statement of Change is to obtain a healthier lifestyle and one of the steps is to run a half marathon. Well, to train for a half marathon, the person will need to eliminate the equivalent amount of activity from the rest of their life. People don't find time. *They modify activities.* Activities might be sitting, watching TV, scrolling on one's cell phone, sleeping, playing, or working. One way to get a handle on one's rhythms of life is to watch one's own life and gather data, including all of one's activities in a typical week.

Some inventory is readily accessible. Like stock in showroom or on the floor, some skills or models or well-fitted rhythms are already in a person's everyday life. But some inventory is in the stockroom: accessible, but it will take a bit more effort to get to. Some skills might be rusty; a person might have foundational knowledge, but it's a bit outdated; there might be a perfect model, but it will take a phone call or two and a specific request.

Investors

A plan has a better chance of success when there are personal investors. An investor is a person who will sacrifice something of value to invest in another's life, providing stabilizing and energizing resources especially in this time of change.

When I was working on my PhD, I had a team of investors. I sent them weekly emails. They sent me random notes. At two different points, I wanted to quit the program. They wouldn't let me. Not without a fight, anyway. They were not financial contributors, but they encouraged, prayed, conversed, and provided appropriate pressure. They spent leisure time with me, listened to me, processed ideas with me, accompanied me on educational trips, and helped out with home repairs. What investors are in the parishioner's life that can be part of the plan to help carry it through to completion?

Investors should be willing to have conflict with the parishioner. I have found that if people are not willing to fight *with* you over the most important things, then neither will they fight *for* you. Sometimes fighting *for* feels like fighting *with*. As a result, investors should be ones whom the parishioner is willing to trust deeply.

Finally, investors often need to be recruited with a direct and specific request for help. "I am attempting to make a change in my life. I need your help. Would you please consider . . . ?" This might include childcare, meal preparation, coaching, prayer, accountability, or a host of other actions that will contribute to achieving the Statement of Change. As the pastor, you can help provide some emotional distance to see if the request is reasonable and/or appropriate.

Impediments

If the Statement of Change could have come about without speed bumps, that route would already have been taken. As a result, you can assume there will be impediments along the way.

Chapter 6

Some impediments are small. John Maxwell tells the story of a one-inch block that sits in front of a massive steam engine that keeps the engine from moving because the train has no momentum. The one-inch block is an impediment.

Some impediments are large. They might even be important relationships in the person's life. Removing these kinds of impediments could be Statements of Change on their own! For example, "To get a working relationship with my father" can be a Statement of Change with specific action steps and habits that facilitate bringing it about. But it might also be part of a larger Statement of Change to develop multi-generational relationships in one's family. Without a functioning relationship with Dad, that can't happen.

Impediments might be a lack of money, skill, or access to technology. Impediments might be concerns among close relationships, especially a spouse. Impediments might be related to timing, such as other events or concerns that need to take higher priority at this moment. Naming impediments is to help assess whether and how they can be removed or their impact lessened.

Increments

The planning phase is about developing steps and habits that will lead to the Statement of Change. Steps head in the desired direction and habits form the necessary dispositions. Depending on the Statement of Change, it will be helpful to anticipate incremental progress. Suppose the Statement of Change involves a change of career and one of the steps is to complete a master's degree in the appropriate field. One of the incremental progress indicators might be a sense of spiritual affirmation. Or the Statement of Change might be a functioning relationship with an adult child. One of the incremental indicators might be a certain amount of communications through the week. A good plan will have indicators as to whether or not the action steps are being effective at moving to the Statement of Change or whether the habits are providing help to strengthen the person's character and resolve to achieve the Statement of Change.

Increments might take on a *negative* form. Rather than being benchmarks to achieve, they are also things to expect. For example, in the midst of almost every Statement of Change that involved forgiveness, I would encourage the parishioner to anticipate spiritual dissonance. Spiritual dissonance might look like low emotional energy or apathy, unnecessary conflict, undefined discouragement, temptation, and so on. When such things are expected, then it confirms that one is likely on the right path.

Steps can be clarified by distinguishing lead measures from lag measures.[5] Lead measures are measurable actions that are meant to achieve other measures. Lead measures are within the control of the person. By the help of the Holy Spirit, a follower of Christ is able to control what they do, say, or allow their mind to dwell upon. While it's last in the list of the nine-fold fruit of the Spirit, self-control is a great testimony to the power of God. On the one hand, lead measures make excellent steps that a person can take. They are specific, can be completed, and should lead to the Statement of Change. On the other hand, lag measures are not within the direct control of the person, but they can be influenced through action.

For example, a person might want to lose fifteen pounds. That goal is certainly measurable, but there might also be factors that keep the goal from happening. A person can't actually control if they lose fifteen pounds. What the person can more reasonably control is how many times they exercise per week, how much water they drink, and what food they buy. In this case, the amount and type of exercise is the lead measure and the person's weight is the lag measure. If the lag measure doesn't follow, then, on the one hand, there might be issues of time (the lead measures are working, but not at the pace predicted), or there might be unexpected factors (the lead measures are working, but other factors have offset their impact). On the other hand, a change of plan might be indicated. Finally, the lag measures might need to be changed.

Steps can act like lead measures, and increments can act like lag measures. Increments are expectations that can either confirm or deny whether the steps are leading to the Statement of Change, though they might be outside the parishioner's control. Of course, increments could be mistaken, but they help to guide the pastor's action in the next step of the kairos moment.

Write It Out

Before the plan is finished, it should be written down and a copy made. Keep a copy for yourself and have the parishioner keep a copy. The form of the copy

Chapter 6

depends on what will be best for the parishioner. They might prefer a chart with descriptions and deadlines. They might prefer a time triangle with the steps and habits written into it. The time triangle has the ability to capture steps, habits, and the Statement of Change all at a glance. The written plan is essential because it will facilitate communication in the action and accountability phase.

BASIC PLAN

Statement of Change:

   I want to overcome some anxiety that is prevalent every fall.

Keystone Habit:

   I will spend five minutes journaling about things I'm grateful for on a daily basis.

   I will be disciplined in Sunday worship.

Steps:

1. I will rearrange my work schedule for Sunday availability.
   a. I will speak to my supervisor by Tuesday.
2. I will purchase a special journal and pen.
   a. I will start going to bed fifteen minutes earlier to be ready to wake earlier.
3. I will turn my typical walking time into a prayer walk. (I will see if Alex will join me every Monday.)
4. Every Friday, I will reflect on whether or not and how I was anxious this previous week.
5. We will meet again on September 30 to talk about how the plan is working.

Conclusion

"Everybody has a plan until they get punched in the mouth."[6] Maybe Iron Mike Tyson's line, forged in the context of boxing, isn't the best way to inform your parishioner that plans will meet with resistance. Maybe it is. Hurdles await the person who is going to enact the plan to change. Don't withhold the truth that once the parishioner goes to work, something will work against them. The plan is in place now, but there's a fist aimed right at their mouth too. But you remain a support. And there are spiritual resources to support along the way. With that in mind, we turn to step 5.

Chapter 7
Action and Accountability

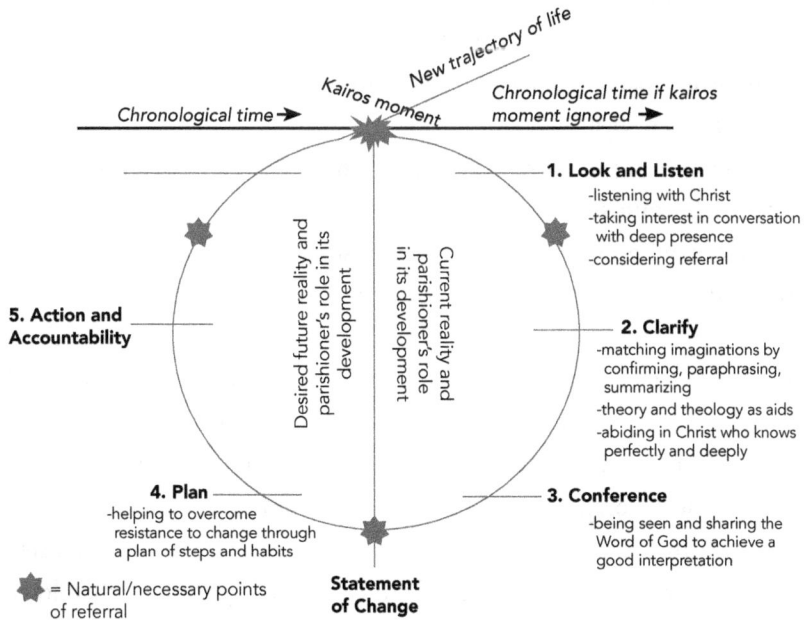

Jesus in the Process

Rich came into my office as my friend. He almost didn't leave that way. Rich, a high-capacity, high-energy volunteer in our church's small groups

Chapter 7

ministry, was navigating a call to ordained ministry. While he was a fully employed professional outside the church, he also made time to volunteer during set hours every week with the discipleship ministry as part of his training. I was his overseer.

Rich was my friend even before we met. The first time he saw me, the new pastor in his church, he marched right up and said, "Do you like steak and do you like swimming?" "Yes and yes." "Great. I've got a barbecue and a pool. When are you coming over?" That was it. Friends for life.

Rich taught me a great phrase: "Front-door friends." When some people are sneaking out the backdoor of your life, making a run for it as your life falls apart, other friends are coming in the front door. They are with you and don't care who knows it. Front-door friends. Rich had been that to many. At one point, Rich needed some front-door friends as he navigated some complex troubles of his own. What a privilege to be that to him. It was because of our relationship that I was overseeing his ministry training. I didn't realize the hazard I was navigating.

The meeting was arranged to confirm, discuss, and address a few issues with Rich's ministry. The meeting wasn't about character or competence but about wisdom. As a pastor, I saw some leadership habits that could eventually sabotage an effective ministry. As *his* pastor and friend, I wanted to see him thrive. About half-way through this perilous meeting, the voice of Christ very gently, very clearly impressed upon me: "You're crushing his spirit." The thoughts were gentle but clear. It was as if Jesus took the agenda from my hands and opened my eyes to the soul sitting before me. Rich's typically bright eyes were dull, and his normally eager shoulders were slumped. But Jesus breathed fresh life into our conversation. Rich stepped into my office a friend and stepped out the same way, even further down the discipleship road, because Jesus stepped into our conversation.

My interaction with Rich exemplifies the Action and Accountability phase. For Rich, a direction had been discerned. A (working) plan was in place. A relationship had been established and tested. Good intentions abounded. *And it almost fell apart.* Stay vigilant at this point in the process.

A Pastor in the Field

"Field conditions!" The phrase from last chapter warned of the unexpected pits on the other side of hurdles for every Statement of Change. Plans are necessary, but action takes place in the field, so often filled with traps, tricks, and mines. Yet the Statement of Change won't be achieved without navigating the field. The plan must be developed but also acted out. Navigating the field is more effective with a guide. The Holy Spirit, present in the conversation, is the guide.

As pastoral shepherds, representing the Great Shepherd, we are humble, not proud (1 Pet 5:2-14). We are grounded in Christ, not in our charisma. We remain a person in need, just as any person before us. Yet with confidence in the faithfulness of Jesus, we are not doubtful but filled with faith and hope, companions on the journey with the compass of love.

Jesus exemplified this difficult role one day when he was called to account by a forced choice (John 8:1-11). The challenge was framed with the highest stakes and hidden sins. Some teachers of the law and Pharisees found a woman accused of adultery and dragged her into Jesus's presence, demanding his response. The Torah prescribed stoning as punishment, but at the time the Romans, not the Jews, enacted capital punishment. The choice was stark: Follow the Law and defy the Romans or defy the Law and submit to the Romans. The challenge to Jesus was brought to a point: "What do you say?" (John 8:5 CEB). But Jesus provides a pastoral response to this either/or confrontation. First, he humbles the demanding mob: "Whoever hasn't sinned should throw the first stone." Second, he pardons the woman redemptively. "Go, and from now on, don't sin anymore" (John 8:7, 11 CEB). The mob used the woman as a trap, but Jesus wouldn't condemn her. Jesus says no to the Pharisees and teachers. Jesus says no to a forced choice. Jesus says no to a life of sin. *But he says yes to the woman.*

Pastoral Posture in Accountability

The pastor in the accountability phase can likewise feel caught between two impossible options. The person has, perhaps, tripped up with a step or two. Perhaps the plan is all but defunct. But they remain oriented toward the change God is bringing. Or possibly the person has given up and is settling back into their previous life. But God's vision remains the same! By identifying with each set of characters from the stoning scene, the pastor can begin to form a pastoral approach to accountability. Just like the mob in John's story, the pastor has failed and fallen before. Be humble, not harsh. Just like the guilty woman, we, too, will give an account for our actions. Be gentle, not severe. But just as Jesus held the line without condemning the woman, so do we guide the person through the minefield of action toward the Statement of Change.

My dad loved the hymn "Our Great Savior." It's easy to tell why. It testifies to Jesus's tenacious faithfulness and tender friendship through the traffic and fear of life. My dad testified to this very Jesus who never left him, even after a life-altering cancer diagnosis. In the words of the hymn, "saving, helping, keeping, loving," Jesus truly was with my dad to the end! Just as Jesus was present to Rich and me, it is Jesus we need to guide us through accountability because it is Jesus who the person needs through the treacherous path. Beyond my dad's endorsement, the first line of each verse of J. Wilbur Chapman's hymn beautifully forms the pastor's work in accountability:

- "Jesus! what a friend for sinners!"
- "Jesus! what a strength in weakness!"
- "Jesus! what a help in sorrow!"[1]

Jesus, what a friend for sinners! "Foes will mean you harm. Fans won't tell you the truth. You want *friends*." I can't remember who gave me the advice, but it stuck. Friends care about you enough to tell you the truth. Pastor: In the accountability phase, you must work to discern and tell the truth as a *friend*. If you agree with the Statement of Change and affirm the plan, then the truth is a yes to the person and a no to actions (or inactions) that would lead to harm; no to giving poor effort to the steps; no to abandoning the necessary habits, and no to giving up if the steps are not immediately successful. It is not easy to be a friend, but remember that you are friends with Jesus personally and through Jesus with the parishioner!

Jesus, what a strength in weakness! But you are not *simply* a friend. The accountability step also requires a pastor, a spiritual guide. There is only so much motivation and strength and courage that you can pass on through your own relational qualities. But you have been equipped with the sacrament, the body and blood of Christ, which is a means of grace. You have been called and ordained to serve a priestly role, presenting and ministering the teaching and spiritual practices that God uses to change hearts and lives.

As the accountability phase progresses, the pastor may and must minister the sacrament of Holy Communion. On the path of new habits and difficult steps to a new reality, the parishioner will need sustenance. Christ is the sustenance! You are serving, ministering Christ. Will Willimon writes, "During the church's first two centuries, pastoral care stressed the sustaining of souls through the vicissitudes of life in an often hostile world. Sustaining and supportive acts such as the Eucharist and unction provided the community with the sustenance it needed to live during difficult times."[2] Serve Communion and anoint with oil! Claim and use the pastoral tools unique to the pastor!

Jesus, what a help in sorrow! The Pharisees and legal experts brought the woman caught in adultery to Jesus to see if he would condemn her. The parishioner might drag himself or herself to you, seeing if you will condemn them, too. Steps not completed, habits half-started, and shortcomings keenly felt. They throw themselves in the dirt and effectively look up, asking, "What do you say?" In the face of sorrow, Jesus is a help! He does not condemn; he does not break bruised reeds.

But at the same time, some sorrow is godly. The parishioner may offer true confession of actual sin—perhaps sin committed and perhaps sin by leaving something undone. As Christ's under-shepherd, you will minister Christ through the hearing of confession and the pronouncement of forgiveness. Distinguish between worldly sorrow and godly sorrow as the prophet from God. Discerning as God's prophet and pronouncing forgiveness as God's priest is spiritual therapy for the soul.

When my wife was in labor, one of the best therapies I could provide was counterpressure. As Heather's body was preparing to give birth to a child, the internal pressure was mounting. To help relieve the pain, I would press as hard as I could against her lower back with a flat hand or the length of my arm. Accountability is a similar effect. The pressure applied can't be sharp and painful, but there should be some pressure to counteract other forces against the parishioner. Too much pressure will crush the spirit. Too little pressure will be a waste of effort. The midwife knew how much pressure to apply; she helped me learn how to listen to Heather and adjust to the moment. Keep in mind that Jesus is present to help you provide the right care to his beloved child in your care.

Accountability on the Path

I'm not a cross-country runner. I learned that when I was about ten years old. A trail had been marked around the perimeter of our town's elementary school. It was about a mile in total distance. The final class of the day was canceled for anyone who wanted to run the lap. I signed up. Well into the second half of the journey, behind the "woods" (which were really about a dozen trees in the back corner of the lot), the trail became complete mud. It was slick and steep. It would take careful navigation to make it through without a wipeout.

I wiped out.

An older student took it upon himself to be my coach. He was all motivation and no method. Without the slightest measure of malice, he looked in my face: "Did that look slippery to you?" My confusion prompted him to repeat the question. "Did that look *slippery* to you?" I knew the answer he wanted, but it wasn't the answer that my muddy clothes revealed. I shook my head. "Keep on going! Keep running!"

So, I did. I kept running. I didn't win. But I learned a lesson. Motivation alone can't change the nature of the trail. We might think "mind over matter" can beat any challenge, but sometimes the reality is "mud under sneakers." The previous chapter was about planning a path. Accountability is about keeping a person on the path and navigating the mud.

Accountability can take place only once action has been taken, once a person has started down the path. If the habits haven't been attempted and the steps haven't been started, then accountability is not the right action. If the person is not willing to form personal habits or attempt their own plan, then the there's no account to give. Their life will remain relatively unchanged. At the same time, accountability is not like scoring a test. Once a test is turned in, the answers can't be changed. Accountability is more like giving feedback during an ongoing project to keep the project and the parishioner going.

Because action must be taken before accountability begins, scheduling the accountability conversation can happen in one of two ways. One option is to require the parishioner to schedule the next meeting only once they have finished a certain number of steps and have given a good-faith effort to the habits. (This appointment could be made after two weeks or two months or longer, depending on the personality and motivation of the parishioner.) The other option is to schedule the next meeting that will serve as a kind of accountability in itself to encourage action. Make sure to follow through with this appointment only after confirming action has been attempted. Determine what kind of support is most helpful to the parishioner, but remember that accountability can only take place once action has been taken. If no action is taken and no accountability can be provided, encourage the parishioner to tweak the plan, but be careful to avoid a rut of ongoing meetings without any significant action being taken.

Staying on the path takes receiving nourishment, avoiding ditches, strengthening the walker, and/or changing the path's conditions. Let's explore these four accountability efforts.

Finding the Parishioner's Place

Accountability starts with clarity on the step being taken. This is why having a written copy of the plan (see previous chapter) is so important. A written plan helps to make things as clear as possible and for there to be little dependence on memory. It's important to use the *very same sheet* on which the plan was written so that the steps don't change, unless intentionally. If the plan is a moving target, then it won't be helpful and might be unhelpful. If adjustments are made, consider writing them on the plan by hand so that the modifications are clear.

Chapter 7

Accountability needs to start with a mutual understanding of reality. Start by drawing the following matrix for the completed action. Every step might not warrant a full analysis, but certainly the most important ones do, and it might take some practice with simpler steps to use the tool well.

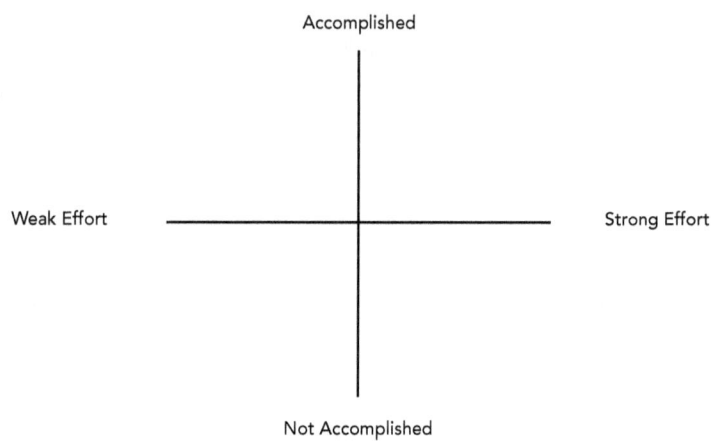

Accountability Matrix

The Accountability Matrix allows a specific step or habit to be positioned clearly. First, was the step accomplished? Was it attempted but not accomplished? While steps can be more clearly accomplished, habits are ongoing. So when considering habits, focus on whether the plan to perform the habit has been followed. For example, if daily prayer is to become a habit, did the person follow their prayer regimen? Or did they not follow their plan? How frequently was the habit or discipline practiced? Second, how strong an effort was given to the step or habit? Notice that the matrix allows for a continuum. The continuum for "Effort" will be more subjective than for "Accomplished."

It's important at this phase to resist the urge to put your own mark on the chart or to provide too strong an opinion. It's *not* your job to chart the actor's efforts and the steps' accomplishment. It's *the parishioner's* job to do so. Of course, you might listen, clarify, and conference to help them discern reality, but discerning reality is *their* work. Watch for whether parishioners are too eager to let themselves off the hook or to critique themselves unfairly.

Action and Accountability

(There is a key difference between accountability for the parishioner and reviewing a person whom you oversee in ministry, whether paid staff or volunteer. In the kairos process, you are a pastor-friend of the parishioner; you are not a pastoral supervisor of an employee. While this matric tool might be used in the oversight role, a different intensity is necessary. In this case, the overseer's opinion carries more weight.)

Once the parishioner charts the step or habit, then accountability becomes clearer, as summarized in the following diagram.

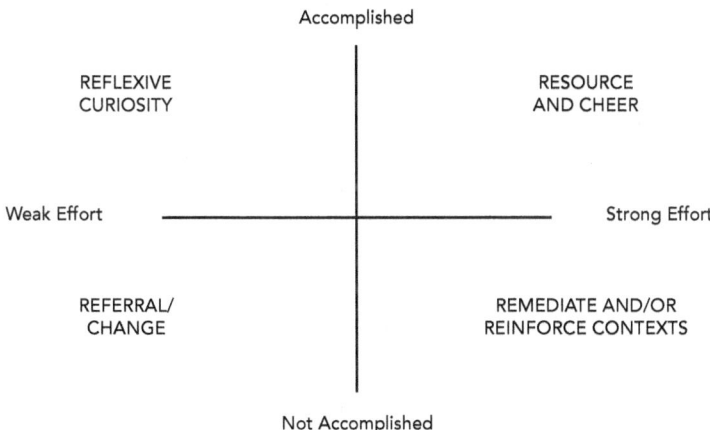

Appropriate Form of Accountability

Let's look at each of these quadrants.

Top Right: Strong Effort
Step/Habit Accomplished: Nourish on the Path

If the parishioner marks the top right quadrant, accountability means *nourishing the parishioner to keep them on the path*. Accountability means to *Resource and Cheer* the parishioner. Most specifically, encourage the new *identity* being formed through the steps and habits. How is Christ being formed? What fruit is the parishioner seeing? What fruit are you seeing in them? How are they forming courage and faithfulness by following through on the steps

Chapter 7

with good effort? What kind of person are they becoming through the habits? Just as you facilitated the plan, but the parishioner designed it, help the parishioner to see what God is doing in their own life by asking questions and reflecting answers. Finally, confirm that the steps and habits are still leading toward the Statement of Change. Keep the goal in mind. Don't neglect Holy Communion as a means of grace and as a way to keep Christ at the center of change. Communion in these meetings may serve to nourish life along the way, the bread strengthening and the cup cheering.

There are two risks the pastor should attend to here. First, there is the risk of completing steps and developing habits without making progress toward the Statement of Change. Being successful at an ineffective plan is like racing on a stationary bike: all tempo, no traction; legs pumping, progress limping. Recall from chapter 6 the increments that were discerned and named. Keep checking the benchmarks to see that progress is really happening.

Second, there is the risk of changing the plan too quickly. The parishioner might want to speed things up or leap over certain steps. If the risk of the above paragraph was the parishioner becoming complacent, the risk here is for the parishioner to become discontented. Your vantage point here is perspective. You are able to recall the whole system as a whole that was developed and can encourage patience and commitment to the plan. If the plan keeps changing simply out of impatience, the parishioner will be cynical of changing the plan, even when changes to the plan really do need to take place.

Think about it like this: Are you impatient with the shower? In your own home you know the right place to turn the dial and roughly how long you need to wait for the desired temperature to be reached. In a hotel or another person's home, it takes some time to find the dial's right setting. If you're not patient in these times, you will overcorrect: turning the dial too hot before it has had time to heat up or turning it too cold before it has had time to cool down. It takes time to know when the dial's setting is in full effect. Likewise, some plans will take time to reveal the progress that's happening beneath the surface. Don't rush to change the settings before the plan has had time to take effect.

Only after patience and persistence should the plan be changed, and only after the plan has been changed and tried, should the Statement of Change be reconsidered. Keep in mind the benefit of good habits through this process. Even if the steps aren't achieving the desired change, the habits are forming a stronger character.

Top Left: Weak Effort
Step/Habit Accomplished: Avoid Ditches beside the Path

If the parishioner marks the top left quadrant, accountability means to engage in *Reflexive Curiosity* in order to *avoid ditches beside the path*. What led to the steps being completed? Perhaps there was momentum or support that hadn't been anticipated. Perhaps support came from investors or unforeseen resources. Perhaps the steps were sufficiently easy that less effort was needed. If the parishioner is ready, add a challenge or reinforce the steps that are to come. Consistent effort is essential, or little change will be achieved.

On either side of the path at this point are two ditches: perfectionism and cynical apathy. This quadrant provides unique opportunities for spiritual reflection. First, analyze the effort. If energy was withheld, delve more deeply.

"Excellence is a sign of care." Karen said the words as she was putting the final, detailed touches on a conference presentation she was doing at our local church. Karen loved our church and was offering an excellent teaching on relationships. Always one to ignore the details until necessary, I was struck by her words. "Excellence is a sign of care." She was focused on removing any distraction and promoting every cue so that each detail would help the attender to keep focused and for *them* to give *their* best effort. Excellence was mutual accountability. If she gave her best, they would be encouraged to do their best, too. If she gave her best, she could encourage them to do so, too.

What's the relationship between excellence and effort? Excellence is giving your best effort in the proper order. If I put my best effort into writing to the neglect of my children, I haven't achieved excellence. If I give my best effort to my family to the neglect of my work and my own (healthy) interests, then I haven't achieved excellence. When I was completing my PhD, I was trying to prioritize full-time studies, full-time work, full-time family. I'm proudest of my lowest grade. That semester, I believe I had my life properly ordered. I now have the privilege of training pastors and leaders who are already in ministry. Some of them are very conscientious students who need reminding that they might earn an 'A' in a class, but it is not the *best* grade

Chapter 7

they could earn. The best grade might be a 'B+' to keep life and relationships in proper order.

Properly ordering one's life is complex. It is also a moral act. Proper ordering of one's life can only be done with God's help, which includes learning and following God's plan in God's power. (Which is exactly what we're trying to do with the Plan and now Accountability!) Without following God's plan in God's power, people will either sacrifice the best for the good enough (which is backwards) or they may take little to no action. The pastor might need to speak an encouraging word here. Giving one's best during a difficult time, even if it is not to the parishioner's own sense of perfection, might be discipline taking root in the parishioner's life! It might truly have been the best a person could do while maintaining a properly ordered life.

Why this discussion about excellence? Because a person may keep from giving good effort if they cannot achieve perfection. However, if it is something the true God has given me to do, then I must strive for excellence even if perfection is not a reality. The true God forbids us from building idols. Some idols demand more than the true God (perfectionism). Some idols demand less than the true God (cynical apathy). The true God does not require one day of work a week. Neither does the true God conform to our desires.

Now, not everyone is as high capacity as Karen. She was putting together details and cues that I hadn't even considered. But I was able to implement the value for the next event I planned. Excellence is a personal act in the context of God's plan with God's power. As a result, the plan might take a more challenging step or a new attitude toward other steps not yet taken (or retaking steps with a new value).

Bottom Right: Strong Effort
Step/Habit Not Accomplished: Change Steps, Strengthen the Walker, or Change the Path's Conditions

If the parishioner marks the bottom right quadrant, accountability means to *build guardrails along the path: Remediate and/or Reinforce Contexts*.

The risk here is *frustration*. The parishioner is giving effort, but steps are not being completed, and, as a result, the Statement of Change is drifting. There is a natural expectation that sufficient effort and a good plan and a desirable outcome will combine for appropriate motivation.[3] But if one of these factors is missing, motivation can wane. When a parishioner has a good plan (Plan) and a desirable outcome (Statement of Change), but their effort is not sufficient for completing steps, then motivation can drop.

Accountability, keeping the person on the path, will include one or a combination of changing the steps on the path, adding support for the walker, or changing the path's conditions. (A person may have withheld effort because of fear, which might have emerged in the Top Left quadrant. Perhaps they reached the precipice of the step but then didn't take it. The following accountability can also be applied in that situation.)

First, consider changing the steps on the path. If there is sufficient effort, consider altering the step. I grew up in the Ottawa Valley in Canada. We had ice for four months of the year. To walk on ice, you should take shorter steps and try to keep your weight in a straight line—as if you have a stick keeping your shoulder, hip, knee, and foot aligned. You step with intentionality. Likewise, while a dry path allows for a long stride, a shorter step is safer on a slippery path. If there is effort, but the step isn't being accomplished or the habit isn't taking root, ask if it can be broken down into shorter steps.

Second, see about adding strength or support to the walker. Sometimes this is simply an encouraging word. The step really is within their stride and they just need to go for it! Sometimes this is reminding a person about skills or resources at their disposal. In the previous chapter we did an inventory of skills, models, knowledge, and rhythms. Can any of these be deployed? If they already have a "walking stick," then they should use it. Finally, strength can be added through a companion on the path. Take a look at the list of investors who were documented in the previous chapter. Can any of these investors accompany the parishioner along the way? Perhaps this looks like daily chats or check-ins or accompaniment during a tough conversation or specific intercessory prayer.

Finally, consider how the path's conditions can be changed. Under the right conditions and over time, a muddy path will dry. In the waiting, God can be forming a new disposition in the parishioner, especially if habits are ongoing. Time is not an enemy; it is the context of change. Time is a gift. Sometimes waiting for the path to dry makes for a wiser walker.

Chapter 7

We can also be more proactive in changing the path's conditions. A path's conditions may change not only with time but also with treatment. An icy path will dry out with some salt or become gritty with some sand. A steep path might need a handrail. What structures can be built? Perhaps others are recruited to the change process by relieving pressures (e.g., so the person in the kairos process can work less hours), taking extra responsibility for a time (e.g., making more meals), or giving up certain freedoms that are prohibitive to the parishioner making progress to the Statement of Change (e.g., going without a cell phone or internet technology or alcohol in the home).

Prayer is one of the practices that can change the conditions on the path. A muddy path, an icy ledge, a steep hill—sometimes these obstacles represent spiritual barriers that can be addressed by the means of grace, which include prayer, thanksgiving, searching the scriptures, and the habit of fasting. Consider spending a whole conversation simply in intercessory prayer together, asking God to change a path's conditions by changing hearts, opening minds, giving courage, and granting favor and mercy.

Bottom Left: Weak Effort
Step/Habit Not Accomplished: Second Try or New Guide

If the parishioner marks the bottom left quadrant, accountability means considering *Referral or a significant Change*. The bottom left quadrant is the default position. If a person doesn't follow up for accountability, this is the quadrant to which they will drift. If the person no longer sufficiently values the plan or your influence, they will likely simply stop scheduling appointments. They will self-select out of the kairos process. In this case, it is tempting to increase *your* effort, to schedule appointments, and to find new ways to motivate; but a very helpful rule for the pastor is this: You can never work harder than the parishioner to achieve change in *their* own life. If the parishioner schedules a conversation and they place themselves in this quadrant, then consider techniques from Top Left (avoiding ditches) or Bottom Right (adding strength). It might be the case that the person remains motivated to the Statement of Change. In this case, they should be encouraged to give a good effort to attempt the steps and implement the habits. A change of attitude can be effective at attempting the plan with good effort.

But if a good-faith attempt simply isn't an option, then it is time for referral. Perhaps the pastor-parishioner relationship is no longer effective at achieving change because influence has been lost. Though the plan was wise and the Statement of Change was right, effort and accomplishment aren't happening. Or perhaps the parishioner has grown tired, even apathetic, possibly clinically depressed. In this case, if the parishioner is willing, suggest referral, perhaps to another pastor and, if necessary, to another professional. If referral is decided upon, then take at least ten to fifteen minutes to document as clearly and precisely as possible the experience and feelings since the plan was developed. What steps have been attempted, what habits have been started, what impediments have been encountered, and so on. This will be helpful if the person has a change of heart and returns.

Finally, what if the person remains on your heart and mind after they have been referred or the kairos process has stopped? What if the Lord consistently keeps them in your prayers? Consider following up *pastorally*, not as an accountability tactic, but by initiating a *listening* conversation to see what might be happening. Use the following diagram, introduced in the Look and Listen phase to guide your listening. Is something happening in their relationship with God? Are they self-condemning? Are there issues in relationships or their vocation/employment that keep them from giving a good effort?

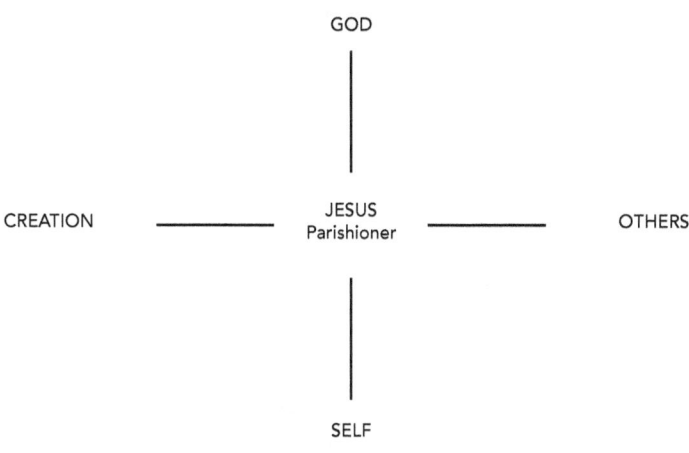

Contexts of Listening

Chapter 7

Here's a summary of the previous section on accountability:

```
                        Accomplished
                             |
   REFLEXIVE CURIOSITY       |    RESOURCE AND CHEER
   -add challenge/step       |    -affirm identity
   -alter values             |    -confirm direction
   -analyze effort           |    -reinforce plan
                             |
Weak Effort ─────────────────┼───────────────── Strong Effort
                             |
   REFERRAL/CHANGE           |    REMEDIATE AND/OR
                             |    REINFORCE CONTEXTS
   -change attitude          |
   -change action            |    -add power
   -change guide             |    -alter context
                             |    -analyze step
                             |
                      Not Accomplished
```

Summary of Accountability Postures
and Possible Actions

Conclusion

Early in my ministry, I made a friend. It surprised me. I wasn't expecting this person to be my friend. We started working on a ministry project together. My friend was eager but a bit shy. We developed a plan, and he took responsibility for a few of the actions. After a week or so, I went to check up on how he was doing with his tasks. He hadn't done anything. I was so frustrated! I had been working ahead, but he had been lagging behind. My frustration slipped off my back, down my arm, and was now being worn on my sleeve. "You haven't done anything? Well, are you going to do any of the work?" I asked. He replied somewhat nonchalantly: "Probably not." The words stung and stuck, so I spun on my heel and slipped away. It was good that I did because I don't know how I might have responded. What I was witnessing was actually a deep problem in my friend's life, one that kept him from making much progress for a few years. In making the friend, I had neglected the pastoral role. Was it my fault that he stayed stuck? No. It was my opportunity, however, to see a bit beneath the surface. I needed to stay a pastor.

While it is both, Action and Accountability is more art than science. It starts and stops with the art of pastoral ministry. Your effectiveness will be connected to the vibrancy of your own relationship with the Great Shepherd. So don't neglect it! You need the Spirit to guide you as you guide others.

One of the most important factors in transformation in the counselor-client relationship is just that: the relationship.[4] The Action and Accountability step puts technique and theory into effective practice under the spirit of pastoral friendship. When done well and by God's grace, the Statement of Change is accomplished and the kairos change is likely to take effect. But a final step remains. The pastor-parishioner relationship doesn't end after accountability. The final step helps to safeguard the relationship and also to enrich the ministry of the congregation under the care of the pastor.

Chapter 8

Follow Up

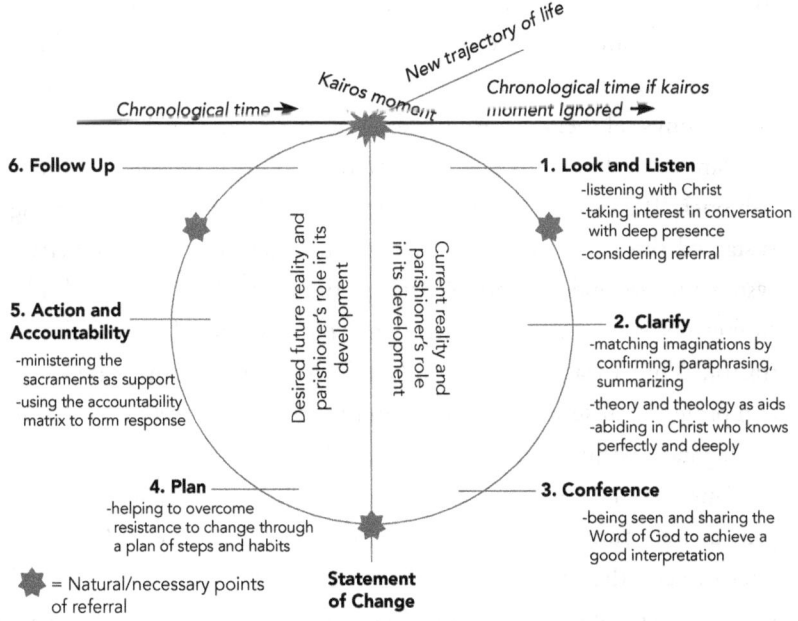

Being Right-Behind Those Who Might Feel Left-Behind

"Living One-Handed in a Two-Handed World." That was the name of the pamphlet the nurse pressed into my right hand as I walked out of the

Chapter 8

hospital. From the tip of my fingers to the crest of my elbow, my left arm was bandaged. Just a few days before, I had cut my left pinky finger while washing dishes. I knew it was bad as soon as it happened, but I didn't know how bad. I had severed the artery, nerve, and tendon. The fading zigzag scar across the digit still brings the surgery to mind, and the slight bend in the finger reminds me of the rehabilitation.

Rehabilitation. The pamphlet was just the beginning. The nurse told me how important it was to do my exercises to reclaim mobility and strength in the finger. But here was the problem: The accident and urgent surgery took place in Colorado where I had been attending a family wedding. Now we needed to begin the two-thousand-plus mile drive back to Ontario, Canada. The first few days were critical to regain as much functioning as possible. On the road, I could begin to do passive exercises—moving the healing finger with my other hand. But when we got back, I had no scheduled follow up and no physical therapist. All I had was a pamphlet.

Similar feelings might emerge at this point of the process for the parishioner. The process is complete, and a new form of living is taking root, sustained through certain habits. But until now there has been structured, systematic pastoral support. What will the new relationship look like? The shift can be similar to my experience as Colorado drifted away in the rearview mirror. While I was leaving behind all the medical expertise, case knowledge, and professional support that I had in the crisis, I was feeling *left behind*, like the regular rhythm of life would pass me by.

But I had lots of resources. The best resource was my wife, Heather. She provided encouragement, accountability, and perspective. When I woke up after surgery, the nurse said, "Did you have any good dreams?" I had been reading a biography of Dietrich Bonhoeffer, so my response made sense to me: "I dreamed I was part of the confessing church, fighting the Third Reich." However, it made no sense to the nurse. "Ohhhhhhkay," she replied in a delayed voice, processing if I needed some other kind of care. Heather smiled, "It's just the book he's reading. He's OK." She couldn't do the exercises on my behalf, but as the new rhythm unfolded, she was with me.

The relationship between pastor and parishioner can be similar. The parishioner might be feeling left behind as the process they have gone through is now in the rearview mirror. Up until now, the pastor has been alongside the parishioner in this journey. The pastor has listened, clarified, conferenced. The pastor has coached, encouraged, and held the parishioner accountable. The necessary shift is from being *beside* to being *right behind*. The pastor remains a support and encourager and intercessor. The parishioner might be feeling left behind, but the pastor reminds the parishioner that they are behind them, cheering them on. The pastor will remain their *pastor*.

At the same time, the parishioner needs ongoing support. They need people who will journey with them. Pastors can't accompany so closely all their parishioners, but all Christians needs the support of the church—the worshipping community among whom they belong and to whom they are responsible. Just as Heather was a support to me, so does the parishioner need the support of the church. And just as my recovery was not in order to bade farewell to my wife and to forget my responsibilities as a father, so is the parishioner to take up responsibility and ministry in and as the church. Even if the Follow Up step has emerged out of referral, the same work applies: The parishioner needs the support of the church and needs to find meaningful and appropriate ministry in and as the church. The experience of each parishioner might be different, but the importance of reconnecting with the church remains a lifeline.

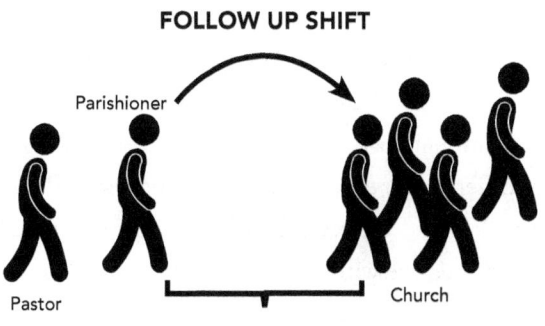

Follow Up Shift

Chapter 8

Navigating Relational Spaces

The first action of follow up is to shift the relational space that has formed between the pastor and parishioner. In a Facebook meme that went viral, on a colorful background was written, "The only thing I haven't told my therapist is that I honestly wish we could be best friends." A therapist can't be a best friend. It would undermine the nature of the relationship. But what about the pastor? In conversation, the pastor is a type of friend. During the kairos process, the relationship between the pastor and parishioner has deepened. It can't help but deepen. The practices of listening, clarifying, and conferencing disclose previously hidden parts of each other's lives, and the practices of planning, acting, and holding accountable have involved highs and lows, losses and wins. A kind of bonding is not only natural but also spiritual—the Spirit has worked in the relationship. While a pastor can be one type of friend, the pastor can't be best friends to everyone in the church. Attempting to be best friends with too many people in the church will undermine the possibility of leading the body. The pastor can likely be best friends to one or two people—and they may or may not be in the church. (If the pastor's best friend is in the church, then addressing possible dual relationships will be essential to faithful leadership.) Yet through the kairos process the pastor has acted as a friend, and perhaps the pastor has acted as the best friend the parishioner has ever had. Since maintaining this relationship in its current form is not possible, the relational space must be shifted.

In his book *The Search to Belong*, Joseph Myers outlines four different kinds of relational spaces: Public, Social, Personal, and Transparent.[1] Each space has different expectations and commitments. Public space unites people with mutual shared interests. Here's an example. Just after getting married, my wife surprised me with Pittsburgh Steelers tickets. We joined with 68,398 other Steelers fans to cheer on the Black and Gold. For the duration of the game, we were all in Public space. We talked strategy, high-fived, shouted at the refs, and cheered the Steelers in unison. However, when the game was over, so was our relationship. We actually became competitors trying to exit the stadium's parking! The relationships were easily navigated.

Social space is a sorting space. It is a kind of friendly friendship. It is the relational space where we try to craft the image we want others to see. If you post pictures on social media, you might take several of the same shot before you get the right image. Social space is like the carefully curated set of photos that you provide to other people as they are getting to know you. Social space is a place to show your best self.

Here's another way to think about social space. Have you ever picked up a hitchhiker? I have on a couple occasions, but not always. When I have, it is because I felt a prick in my conscience to go back and pick them up. Most of the time, however, I don't have space in my vehicle and just drive on by. It isn't awkward. Now, imagine you see your neighbor hitchhiking. You make eye contact and yet you drive on by. How would you feel? How might your neighbor feel? What would it be like the next time you ran into each other as you were checking the mail? Social space is like the space you occupy with neighbors. You are expected to give—and you can expect to receive—small favors.

If social space involves being critical about what "photos" you allow others to see, personal space gives over a much larger stack of pictures. It's like giving your cell phone over and allowing someone to look through it. The expectations and commitments are higher. Personal space is about being front-door friends. When people are sneaking out the backdoor of your life, people with whom you are in personal space are coming in the front door. And they expect the same of you.

Finally, transparent space means a relationship where nothing is hidden. Everything is disclosed (or could be disclosed) and no secrets are intentionally withheld. This is the space of best friends.

We often navigate spaces seamlessly. I didn't wonder if a Steelers fan (public space) was going to invite my wife and me out to dinner after the game (social space), but when a church member (public space) asks my family over for a meal (social space), it's usually an easy yes. And if we don't connect again for a year, we don't think much about it. Likewise, potential friends (social space) normally earn trust with each other by disclosing elements of their lives freely and mutually (personal space).

But sometimes navigating spaces is more difficult. To complicate matters, the church often blurs relational spaces. As a gathered community

Chapter 8

(public space), we discuss profound and personally challenging issues (transparent space). As small groups (social space?) we disclose to people with whom we otherwise might not be friends (personal space) and from whom we might need deep support (transparent space). For our purposes, the pastor-parishioner relationship during the kairos process might have elements that normally mark a very deep friendship (personal or transparent space), but now the relationship needs to return to a different space (perhaps more like social space or public space). Having a misunderstanding at this point risks the whole relationship. So while this transition can be challenging and even a bit awkward, it is important to protect the relationship even while it is being navigated. If the kairos process was laid out early on the in process as suggested, then the Follow Up step has been anticipated. It's part of the unfolding plan. If not, then it is helpful to show the parishioner the process they've just come through.

Here is a way of navigating the relational shift.

First, during the follow up conversation, listen for the expectations of the parishioner. The parishioner's expectations can come in the form of questions.

"Will you text me?"

"Can we still get together?"

"What if I need help?"

They can also come in the form of concerns.

"I don't know about returning to school."

"When I see _____, I don't know if I'll make a good choice."

"I just hope I can keep the relationship going strong."

Second, confirm the underlying values of the parishioner's expectations. So, for example, "Will you text me?" might be addressed by saying, "I think that supportive and ongoing communication is important to you." Or, "Can we still get together?" might be addressed by saying, "It sounds like our time together has been meaningful to you. It has been to me too." Apply some of the clarifying skills practiced earlier in the model to make sure that the expectation and its corresponding value are accurately understood.

Third, once the underlying value has been confirmed, then support the parishioner's values while also encouraging actions consistent with the new life they are beginning to live out. "Ongoing communication is essential as you move into a new rhythms and patterns. What might you do to initiate this communication with others?" Or, "Maintaining supportive relationships will be important as you move forward. What relationships do you already have that might become these supports?"

Fourth, be clear about your role: You have been and will continue to be the parishioner's pastor. That doesn't change. As the pastor, enjoy the freedom of this role! While a therapist can't be an ongoing friend to the client, the pastor is free to remain a pastor to the parishioner! At the same time, the pastor is not a private tutor, life coach, or spiritual guru. The pastor is responsible to the church as a body and must work to that end.

Fifth, mutually construct the ongoing relationship. Because of these related responsibilities—to the whole church body and to the church in this particular parishioner—the form of relationship can be constructed between the pastor and the parishioner. For example, you and the parishioner might set a time to reconnect in six weeks for informal, unstructured conversation. Or you might tell the parishioner you will check in with them next quarter or after a certain event or season. Or you can encourage the parishioner to make an appointment with you next month. If you agree to an informal connection, I encourage the pastor to put a reminder in their own calendar so that they do not forget. If a key leader has just gone through a process, I might connect within four to six weeks. If a person who has gone through significant loss has gone through the process, I suggest scheduling a communication near the anniversary of the loss (in addition to other check-ins).

See You in Church!

The relationship is finally navigated by affirming that the local church is the God-ordained community for the parishioner's spiritual growth and ongoing new life. The local church, not the pastor alone, is the community to provide ongoing relational support, communication, accountability, prayer, and intercession. Let's spell this out a little bit more.

Put yourself in the conversation we've just considered. The parishioner is moving into a phase of life with less pastoral support. The stakes are high. When this step isn't navigated well (or is simply neglected), people can leave

Chapter 8

the church. If the parishioner kept church attendance as part of their life or as a specific habit as was suggested, then it is more likely that they will stay in the church. If they have been "taking a break" from church, then it will be more difficult for them to re-engage in the life of the church, but it is still important to work toward reintegration.

There are two common reasons that people leave (or don't return) at this stage of the kairos process. First, they might leave the church because of the sensed relational crater left by the pastor's relational shift. In the process of the kairos conversation, the pastor can become a substitute for the church. The pastoral relationship acts like a kind of spiritual inoculation: It's like friendship with the pastor has made a person immune to spiritual dangers and has guaranteed spiritual health. If the pastor has become a personal church or spiritual experience for the parishioner and the church is already absent, then once the process winds down and the relationship with the pastor shifts, the person essentially left the church weeks or months earlier.

Second, people might leave the church because they don't want things to go back to the way they were. People who have done *this* much work through this process will risk relationships, personal suffering, and even offending others to keep their lives from regressing. Now, in some cases a change of church might be wise and necessary—and may have been part of the plan. In this case, holding the parishioner accountable to finding another church would have been important. Other times, leaving a church (or "taking a break") might be a scheme of the enemy to get the parishioner out of church *for good*. Just when they need supportive and spiritual community, they are leaving it. The Follow Up step helps the parishioner to consider how their life in the church can foster the ongoing transformation that God has brought about through the kairos process. The ongoing life and ministry of the church in worship, prayer, preaching, baptism, and Communion is a vital component to a new rhythm of life. If it was *God* who initiated the kairos moment, then *God* and the things of God will remain part of the new rhythm!

For the pastor, *now*—right now—is a great time to consider your church's systems and structures that serve to integrate, disciple, and place people in Christian community and ministry. *The parishioner finishing the kairos process is one of the people these systems should serve.* Does the church have a step for the person to discover their spiritual gifts or ministry skills? Does the church have a step for the person to be deployed in ministry? Does the church have a step for this person to enter into more relational community? Does the church have disciple-makers who can carry on a shepherding or mentoring role with this person? For the person just finishing the kairos process and who is gifted for leadership, does the church have a leadership training system? Does the church have people who intercede regularly, strategically, and systematically in prayer for others in the church?

These questions about congregational care can be overwhelming. If any of these systems are in place, excellent! Use them as appropriate as part of the Follow Up step to incorporate the person into the life of the church. Any system that already exists is a potential route for the person to take to strengthen their church relationship and belonging.

At the same time, you might be missing a system and can see which area of ministry development deserves attention and resources. Strategy is putting resources behind opportunity. Vijay Govindaran says, "Strategy is about allocating resources *today* to secure a better *tomorrow*"[2] (italics in original). Be strategic! Allow your pastoral care to guide where you should begin allocating resources, including personal and staff time and attention, creative people, and money. As pastor, you have been given authority to lead the church. And the church, in a particular person, is sitting across from you. If these systems are lacking, unclear, or ineffective, face the reality. Allow this person not to be God's condemnation of your leadership, but rather to be God's grace to make it more effective.

Pastoral Authority and the Family of God

Depending on your tradition, you might be ordained or on an ordination track. The ordained person is set aside to lead in the church through preaching, serving the sacraments, and ordering the church. Part of ordering the structure is sending into ministry. Authority is not for the sake of hoarding power, but for authorizing others to act in power. *Authority is to empower right action.* Your pastoral authority, which has been so helpful through the kairos process, is now about encouraging the person to take up responsibility and be part of the life of the church.

Pastoral authority is not *over* another; it is *for* another. Pastoral authority is for the good of the church body to be built up by the ministry of a particular person, and it is for the good of the particular person by ordering their meaningful ministry in the church. St. Augustine describes this kind of authority well. On the anniversary of his ordination, St. Augustine preached a sermon. In it he said, "For you I am a bishop, with you, after all, I am a Christian."[3] Pastor: Here's the bottom line: God didn't bring the person through this kairos process with you by their side in order for them to leave the church! If you are a pastor in your local church, your role is to help order the church by calling people into its ministry. But you do so not strictly from above but as a person who has been called into ministry yourself. Just as it has not been your role to convince the parishioner of your opinion or to share your convictions, neither now is it your responsibility to *convince* the person to find their community and to perform meaningful ministry in the church.

Testify!

The fruit of faithful pastoring is not a bigger church. The fruit of faithful pastoring is more preachers: people who testify to the work of God's word. One of the best first actions of the parishioner in ministering to the church is to testify to the work of God in her or his life through this process. A testimony can be thought of as a brief telling of one's autobiography. When a person can retell their autobiography with Christ at the center and the church as his or her people, then a deep shift has taken place in the heart and mind of the person.[4]

As part of the Follow Up process, ask the person to write out a testimony of the kairos process. The structure is simple. First, briefly describe the kairos moment (or season) that sparked this change. Second, summarize the conferencing process—what did God reveal in this step?—and include, as appropriate, the Statement of Change. (Some statements might not be appropriate to share publicly, so discretion is advised.) Third, describe the work of God in helping to bring about a new rhythm or pattern of life or a decision that is

God-honoring. Finally, describe what you see God doing now or what you anticipate God doing in the future.

The testimony can be shared in a number of ways. Depending on your worship style and pattern, testimony can be shared live or pre-recorded. The testimony can be shared with a small group. The testimony can be shared as part of another person's kairos process. If a person takes the time to write out their testimony, then it can be more easily revised and refreshed for future use. Finally, it can be beneficial to have people share a testimony with others who have gone through the kairos process. A group of four to six people each sharing their testimony can be a fine way to help them refine the testimony itself and to edify the body of Christ.

Blessing

Bless the parishioner as a final act of following up. We have lost the art and meaning of the blessing. It's time to recover it. The Follow Up step is a perfect time to bless the parishioner, to speak words of life and favor into their life. Proverbs 18:21 says that the power of life and death is in the tongue. Your words matter. And your final words matter. After navigating the new relational space, ordering the church as pastor, and calling forth the parishioner's testimony, it is time for a final word of blessing.

The best way to develop a blessing is to use Scripture, tailored to the person before you. Numbers 6:24-26, Psalm 20:4, Psalm 23, Psalm 29:11, Jeremiah 17:7-8, Ephesians 2:8-10 and 3:20-21, and Philippians 2:12-13 are delightful scriptures from which to develop a variety of blessings. It is helpful to memorize a handful of blessings to use in the moment. Also, consider writing out a blessing ahead of this final conversation in order to give to them as a more personal gift.

The world is inundated with words. Text messages, hot takes, Tweets: endless words that have dubious purpose. Most of our people need silence, not more words! But a blessing is a different kind of word. A blessing is a *guiding* word that shields us. A blessing is a *filling* word that satisfies us. A blessing is an *authoritative* word that sustains us. In worship or in pastoral conversations, your final word is a vital word.

Tending to the Pastor: Expectations and Encouragements

The pastor also has a shepherd! Now is the time to be cared for by *Jesus*. Few things run the complement of pastoral care as a complete kairos process. Whether the process has been over a series of meetings or contained in a single conversation, the heart, mind, and spiritual life of the pastor have been put into service. Jesus puts us to use as pastors but does not use us up.[5] Jesus does not drive the pastor into the ground, demanding no rest, relaxation, or reprieve. If you are leading yourself in such a way, then you are doing ungodly things and must change your behavior.

Once a kairos process has finished, take time for the Lord Jesus to tend to your soul. Depending on the process just finished, it might be an hour or two, a day or two, or even a week or two. This is not vacation but a shift in work. Gauge the tasks and schedule before you and determine which will require an atypical amount of your energy. If some tasks will require an especially sharp mind, open heart, or strong sense of self, then consider pushing them until after a recovery period has been completed.

Expect to feel downcast. Especially if the kairos process has been lengthy, intense, or stressful, a period of downtime is often necessary. How strange it feels when there is great accomplishment and the pastor feels down, even depressed! Sometimes this is the effect of adrenaline deprivation. Pastors, like any person, can depend on adrenaline for a season. Once this season is complete, the body detoxifies. It is like the body is wondering where this substance went! Remember and remind yourself that after periods of strain and stress, even if they end in success, we should expect our bodies to recalibrate. Avoid jumping into new high-pressure opportunities in order to feel the rush and a sense of vitality once again. *Feeling downcast is exactly what to expect.* Monitor it, of course, to see that there is reemergence after a period of time, but it is to be expected.

Follow Up

This period of withdrawal—both from acute responsibility and possibly from unsustainable energy sources—is a space for the Holy Spirit to fill in the gap. During this time, allow the Spirit to minister to you through the prayers of others. Here are a few ways. First, ask others to pray for you and receive their prayers. Perhaps this is a small group in your church or another friend in the faith. Second, plan brief times of silence and solitude. Don't simply take it as it comes, but plan for it. It is an appointment with God. Third, enjoy a comfort that God has provided. This might be your home, hobby, or a hamburger. Having a habitat is part of being an embodied creature. Creatures naturally craft certain comforts and human beings are no exception. The point is not to substitute any of these *for* God, but to accept them as gifts *of* God as a kind of rest and recuperation. Fourth, reflect and use a journal to record what you saw God do, what you learned, what you did well, and what you might do differently next time.

Expect for the person to seek you out again or expect others to seek you out because of the person's testimony. A sign of an effective kairos process is not that the person never returns, but that the person *does* return. And that they encourage others to go through a similar process. Because of this likelihood, pay attention to your own need. Consider your own "case load." Not every pastor can handle the same amount of kairos processes at once. Develop a set of best practices that you implement and to which you are held accountable by the authorities to whom you submit, whether a spouse, board, or friend.

Expect to grieve. We can't plan grief. We grieve when grief comes. We can't stop grief and we can't start grief. After a kairos process is completed, there can be a sense of gnawing loss in one's spirit. It might be immediate. It might be several weeks after the intense conversation or kairos process. Grief takes different forms for different people: anxiety, anger, sadness, irritability, and temptation. Be mindful of grief and name it properly.

Finally, it is possible that you might feel bitterness. After going through this process, you might expect a measure of loyalty, service, support, and affirmation from the parishioner. And when it isn't shown, it's easy to feel bitter and frustrated. It's easy to entertain certain thoughts. "I was so helpful to them! Their life is different because of my ministry! Don't they *owe* me?" These are natural feelings. You aren't alone in feeling them. But they are not feelings to dwell upon. They won't sustain your soul or strengthen your spirit. Just as the parishioner has undergone a process, not for himself or herself strictly, but to better serve and lead their family, church, friends, and others for the sake of Christ, so have you helped to facilitate this process not for your own sake. You have done this work for the sake of Christ's transformation of hearts and lives. You have done this as an act of worship. Fortunately, Jesus is a leader who sees every bit of faithful work that others never will see. He knows the time his pastors spend in challenging study, secret prayer, quiet reflection, earnest solitude, and diligent service. Christ knows. And while the parishioner may be disloyal, unhelpful, and disparaging, Christ remains not only a friend to sinners but also a friend to his pastors.

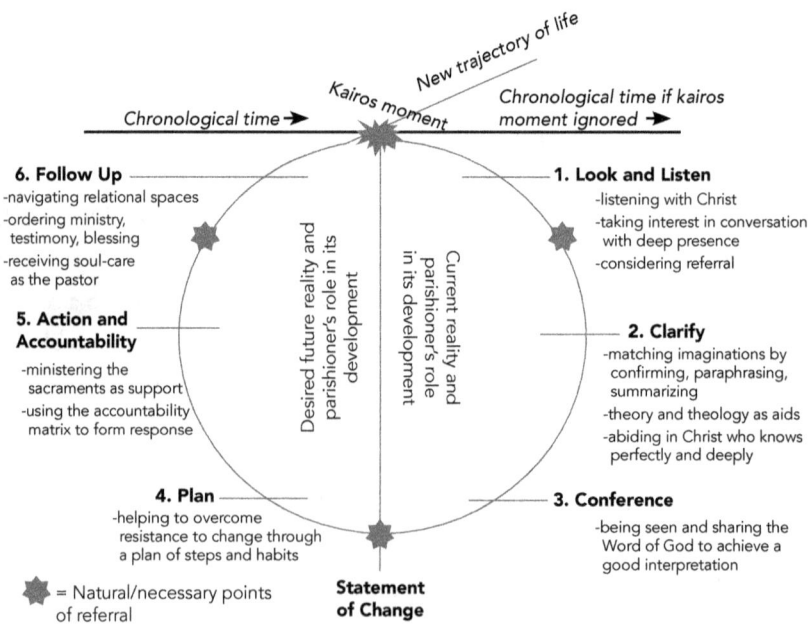

Completed Kairos Process

Notes

Introduction

1. Throughout this book, I will use examples from my own pastoral experience. Details such as names and places have been changed so as to protect identities. Also, some of the examples are composites of more than one example that had significant overlap.

2. As quoted by William Willimon, *Pastor: The Theology and Practice of Ordained Ministry* (Nashville: Abingdon Press, 2002), 60.

3. John Wesley, "The Good Steward," Wesley Center Online, Northwest Nazarene University, accessed April 28, 2020, http://wesley.nnu.edu/john-wesley/the-sermons-of-john-wesley-1872-edition/sermon-51-the-good-steward/.

4. Kenneth L. Carder and Laceye C. Warner, *Grace to Lead: Practicing Leadership in the Wesleyan Tradition* (Nashville: United Methodist General Board of Higher Education, 2016), 86.

5. Throughout this book, I will use the following words somewhat interchangeably: soul, self, well-being, life. Pastoral ministry has traditionally been referred to as the "care of souls." This should not be taken to mean that the pastor cares for some part of the human person ("the soul") while ignoring other parts of the human person ("the body"). Instead, pastors care for the whole of the human person, embodied beings embedded in relationship with God and God's creation. The pastor always has an eye to the person's relationship with God.

1. The Model

1. Peter J. Leithart, *Solomon Among the Postmoderns* (Grand Rapids: Brazos, 2008).

2. For more on proper posture toward the uncontrollability of time and the appropriate posture toward work in Ecclesiastes, see Larisa Levicheva-Joseph, "Ecclesiastes," in *Wesley One Volume Commentary*, ed. Kenneth J. Collins and Robert W. Wall (Nashville: Abingdon Press, 2020), 358–70.

3. Thanks to Dr. Daniel Freemyer for pointing this out to me.

4. See Tim S. Perry, *Mary for Evangelicals: Toward an Understanding of the Mother of Our Lord* (Grand Rapids: IVP, 2006).

5. This also raises the questions of emotions, especially negative emotions, and their relation to the harms one may have suffered, the faith that God is preserving, restoring, building, etc., and the will of the parishioner. For an approach informed both by psychology and theology, see Matthew Lapine, *The Logic of the Body: Retrieving Theological Psychology* (Bellingham, WA: Lexham, 2020).

6. Carl Rogers, *A Way of Being* (New York: Houghton Mifflin, 1980), 142.

7. Arthur Frank, *The Wounded Storyteller: Body, Illness, and Ethics*, 2nd ed. (Chicago: Chicago University Press, 2013). Frank's three-fold typology of restitution, quest, and chaos narratives is very helpful for readers who would continue to research and reflect on narratives in the midst of listening and counsel.

8. See Richard Osmer, *Practical Theology: An Introduction* (Grand Rapids: Eerdmans, 2008). While my structure won't be identical to Osmer's, he is certainly an influence.

2. Look and Listen

1. Ethel Glenn, "A Content Analysis of Fifty Definitions of Listening," *International Journal of Listening* 3, no. 1 (1989): 21–31.

2. Debra L. Worthington and Graham D. Bodie, eds. *The Sourcebook of Listening Research: Methodology and Measures* (New York: John Wiley & Sons, 2017). The authors use the categories of affective, behavioral, and cognitive.

3. Alan Mann, "Why Listening? Considering Contemporary Culture, Christianity, and the Value of Listening," in *Developing Ears to Hear: Listening in Pastoral Ministry, the Spiritual Life, and Theology*, ed. Aaron Perry (Lexington, KY: Emeth Press, 2011), 17–28.

4. Frank Lake, *Clinical Theology* (Lexington, KY: Emeth Press [unabridged edition], 2005), 1:52.

5. See Arthur Frank's concept of the chaos narrative. Arthur Frank, *The Wounded Storyteller: Body, Illness, and Ethics*, 2nd ed. (Chicago: Chicago University Press, 2013).

6. John Wesley, "John Wesley to Miss March, February 26, 1776," Wesley Center Online, The Letters of John Wesley, accessed May 11, 2020, http://wesley.nnu.edu/john-wesley/the-letters-of-john-wesley/wesleys-letters-1776/.

7. John Wesley, "On Visiting the Sick," Wesley Center Online, accessed May 11, 2020, http://wesley.nnu.edu/john-wesley/the-sermons-of-john-wesley-1872-edition/sermon-98-on-visiting-the-sick/.

3. Clarify

1. I owe this phrase to my friend Dr. Joy Moore. She described her work as a professor of preaching as "a practical theologian who works with words."

2. See Mildred Bangs Wynkoop, *A Theology of Love: The Dynamic of Wesleyanism* (Kansas City, MO: Beacon Hill Press, 1972), chap. 6.

3. Lacy Finn Borgo, interview with Aaron Perry, Wesley Seminary Podcast, podcast audio, July 13, 2020, https://soundcloud.com/user-743479271/128-dr-lacy-finn-borgo-spiritual-conversations-with-children.

4. For an excellent application of Family Systems Theory to congregations, see R. Robert Creech, *Family Systems and Congregational Life: A Map for Ministry* (Grand Rapids: Baker Academic, 2019).

5. The pastor's words—expressing the forgiveness of God to the repentant and contrite person—are certainly *more* than therapeutic, but they are not less than therapeutic. God's forgiving heart announced and modeled by the pastor is *real* comfort.

4. Conference

1. Ron Heifetz, *Leadership without Easy Answers* (Cambridge, MA: Harvard University Press), chap. 10.

2. Kevin Watson, "Holy Conferencing: What Did Wesley Mean? (Part 2)," accessed July 14, 2020, https://kevinmwatson.com/2013/07/18/holy-conferencing-what-did-wesley-mean-part-2/.

3. This illustration developed from an illustration by Gabriel Salguero at a chapel service at Indiana Wesleyan University.

4. See Henry Cloud, *Necessary Endings: The Employees, Businesses, and Relationships That All of Us Have to Give Up in Order to Move Forward* (Grand Rapids: Zondervan), chap. 7, for practical wisdom on this subject.

5. William Willimon, *Pastor: The Theology and Practice of Ordained Ministry* (Nashville: Abingdon Press, 2002), 182.

6. See John C. Thomas and Lisa Sosin, *Therapeutic Expedition: Equipping the Christian Counselor for the Journey* (Nashville: B&H Publishing, 2011), chap. 7. Thomas and Sosin provide an excellent, thorough textbook for Christian counseling that may be applied by pastors in counseling situations.

7. The subject of race and racism has become even more important and more sensitive since this section was initially written. My friend and New Testament scholar Dr. Abson Joseph has wise words on the subject: "We need conversations about race, and there is no other conversation like it." This is a wise and insightful reminder to be humble in the practice of hiding. For more on the subject of racism and racial trauma, see Sheila Wise Rowe, *Healing Racial Trauma: The Road to Resilience* (Grand Rapids: IVP, 2020).

8. Willimon, *Pastor*, 200.

9. Dietrich Bonhoeffer, *Life Together* (New York: Harper & Row, 1954), 48.

10. C. S. Lewis, *Weight of Glory* (New York: HarperOne, 2001), 45.

11. Brian Edgar, *The God Who Plays: A Playful Approach to Theology and Spirituality* (Eugene, OR: Wipf & Stock, 2017), 49.

5. Statement of Change

1. William Willimon, *Pastor: The Theology and Practice of Ordained Ministry* (Nashville: Abingdon Press, 2002), 180.

2. Space precludes a deep discussion of forgiveness, but if this is an issue that you face regularly in your pastoral care and counsel, then it might be

an issue that you could study more deeply and more widely. Consider such research as strengthening your clarifying and conferencing work. I highly recommend Gregory L. Jones, *Embodying Forgiveness: A Theological Analysis* (Grand Rapids: Eerdmans, 1995).

3. Sondra Wheeler, *Minister as Moral Theologian: Ethical Dimensions of Pastoral Leadership* (Ada, MI: Baker Academic, 2017), 87.

4. See Scot McKnight's discussion of subversion, including his debt to Eugene Peterson, in *Pastor Paul: Nurturing a Culture of Christoformity in the Church* (Grand Rapids: Brazos, 2019), 147.

6. Plan

1. Christopher Hodgkinson, in *The Philosophy of Leadership* ([New York: St Martin's Press, 1983], 22), explores the difference between nomothetic laws and idiographic laws.

2. The formula for change was first developed by David Gleicher, but Kathie Dannemiller popularized the version of the formula presented here. See S. H. Cady, J. Jacobs, R. Koller, and J. Spalding, "The Change Formula: Myth, Legend, or Lore," *OD Practitioner* 46, no. 3 (2014): 32–39.

3. Charles Duhigg, *The Power of Habit: Why We Do What We Do in Life and Business* (New York: Random House, 2012).

4. This diagram was inspired by Amy Webb's concept, "Time Cones." I have modified the phrase to a time triangle. See Amy Webb, "How to Do Strategic Planning Like a Futurist," *Harvard Business Review*, accessed July 10, 2020, https://hbr.org/2019/07/how-to-do-strategic-planning-like-a-futurist.

5. Stephen R. Covey and Jennifer Colosimo, *The 4 Disciplines of Execution* (Salt Lake City, UT: Franklin Covey, 2004).

6. Mike Berardino, "Mike Tyson Explains One of His Most Famous Quotes," accessed June 23, 2020, https://www.sun-sentinel.com/sports/fl-xpm-2012-11-09-sfl-mike-tyson-explains-one-of-his-most-famous-quotes-20121109-story.html.

7. Action and Accountability

1. J. Wilbur Chapman, "Jesus! What a Friend for Sinners," *Hymns of Faith and Life* (Winona Lake, IN: Light and Life Press; Marion, IN: The Wesley Press, 1976).

2. William Willimon, *Pastor: The Theology and Practice of Ordained Ministry* (Nashville: Abingdon Press, 2002), 172.

3. See Victor Vroom, Lyman Porter, and Edward Lawler, "Expectancy Theories," in *Organizational Behavior 1*, ed. John B. Miner (New York: Routledge, 2005), 94–113. For a brief overview, see "Vroom's Expectancy Theory," Institute for Manufacturing, Cambridge University, accessed July 10, 2020, https://www.ifm.eng.cam.ac.uk/research/dstools/vrooms-expectancy-theory/.

4. See Virginia Todd Holeman, *Theology for Better Counseling: Trinitarian Reflections for Healing and Formation* (Grand Rapids: IVP, 2012), chap. 3: "A Theologically Reflective Counseling Relationship."

8. Follow Up

1. Joseph Myers, *The Search to Belong: Rethinking Intimacy, Community, and Small Groups* (Grand Rapids: Zondervan, 2003). Myers uses the term "Intimate Space," which I replaced with "Transparent Space," following Bobby Harrington and Alex Absalom, *Discipleship That Fits: The Five Kinds of Relationships God Uses to Help Us Grow* (Grand Rapids: Zondervan, 2016).

2. Vijay Govindaran, "Strategy's No Good Unless You End Up Somewhere New," *Harvard Business Review*, accessed December 28, 2020, https://hbr.org/2014/05/strategys-no-good-unless-you-end-up-somewhere-new.

3. St. Augustine, "Sermon 340," https://wesleyscholar.com/wp-content/uploads/2019/04/Augustine-Sermons-306-340.pdf.

4. Scot McKnight, *Open to the Spirit: God in Us, God with Us, God Transforming Us* (Colorado Springs, CO: Waterbrook Press, 2018), 80.

5. I owe this phrase to Dr. Devin Brown.

www.ingramcontent.com/pod-product-compliance
Lightning Source LLC
Chambersburg PA
CBHW050527170426
43201CB00013B/2118